D1517850

The social and economic conditions of
SOVIET FOREIGN POLICY

Soviet Foreign Policy

Its social and economic conditions

Edited by
Egbert Jahn

St. Martin's Press, New York

Copyright © Campus Verlag 1976
Translation Copyright © Allison & Busby Ltd. 1978
All rights reserved. For information, write:
St. Martin's Press, Inc., 175 Fifth Avenue, New York, N.Y. 10010
Printed in Great Britain
Library of Congress Catalog Card Number 77-18229
ISBN 0-312-74836-1
First published in the United States of America in 1978

Library of Congress Cataloging in Publication Data

Main entry under title:
The social and economic conditions of Soviet foreign policy.
    1.   Russia—Foreign relations—1975-   —Addresses,
essays, lectures.   2.   Russia—Economic conditions—1965-
—Addresses, essays, lectures.   I   Jahn, Egbert.
DK274.S65195   327.47   77-18229
ISBN 0-312-74836-1

CONTENTS

1

Four approaches to the analysis of Soviet foreign policy

EGBERT JAHN

Social structure and foreign policy

Any foreign policy of a national government seeks to portray itself as expressing the national interest, the common good of the people as a whole. Scientific analysis, in so far as it provides more than simple ideological justification, strives to penetrate beyond what passes for national interest to the underlying socio-economic interest situation in which the political decision-makers are themselves involved. Since, in spite of the proclamation of popular sovereignty, no nation actually represents a completely homogeneous social unity, but consists of different social groups which look after their interests to a varying degree (in the dual sense of becoming aware of their interests and of actually implementing them), the following basic question poses itself: how do socially dominant interests determine foreign policy? A precondition for the analysis of foreign policy is, accordingly, the analysis of social structure — if the investigation is not to remain limited to the description and classification of foreign policy moves or "non-events".

According to which of the several different theoretical approaches to analysing Soviet social structure one sets out from, one arrives at basically different assessments of Soviet foreign policy. These assessments are usually deduced from social analyses which are themselves rooted in various different social interests. In rarer cases the empirical observation of foreign policy can, on the other hand, lead to a re-examination of basic assumptions about social structure. Today, for example, Chinese foreign policy has caused many people to re-examine thoroughly their idea of

Chinese society. A consensus seems to be emerging that the social relations, and consequently the foreign policy, of the Soviet Union exhibit characteristic differences from the social relations and foreign policy of the capitalist superpowers. Neither those authors who assert that productive relations in the Soviet Union always have been or are once again capitalistic, nor those who generally hold productive relations to be politically irrelevant and overlook them, nor finally those analysts who interpret both Soviet and American society as a post-industrial one, can avoid the need to justify their thesis of a fundamental similarity between American and Soviet foreign policy. Soviet foreign policy can hardly still be treated as *self-evidently* analogous to that of capitalist countries, in the way that British, French and American foreign policy can be viewed as basically alike once the historical and national peculiarities of the aims, instruments and methods of procedure of the individual countries have been emphasised.

Nevertheless, there exists disagreement as to how great the differences and how deep the contrasts are between the foreign policy of the Soviet Union and the countries allied to it, and that of capitalist countries. (The question of the identity or difference between Soviet and Chinese foreign policy on the basis of their basically similar or dissimilar socio-economic relations must be left out of consideration in this essay.) One can distinguish four main tendencies among the theories of Soviet social structure and foreign policy: (i) the institutional marxist-leninist theory of the Soviet type, (ii) the bourgeois élite theory, (iii) theories of recapitalisation and of residual capitalism in the Soviet Union, and (iv) theories of Soviet society as a new kind of social formation which is neither capitalist nor socialist.

The first and second theories start from the assumption that socialism has been achieved in the Soviet Union — either as a model to be imitated or as a terrible example for the rest of the world. The two theories differ in particular in their divergent selections of facts (not to mention false statements of "fact") which either aim at proving the progressive, democratic character of Soviet society and its tendency to economic equality, or, on the contrary, emphasise its backwardness, its dictatorial totalitarian régime and the preservation of socio-economic inequality. Methodologically, both approaches have much in common.

Theories of the third and fourth type do not basically deny the facts with which the bourgeois élite theory refutes the humanistic claims of socialism, but interpret these facts rather as the manifestation of non-socialist or of not yet socialist elements and forms of social relations in the Soviet Union.

The four tendencies

In the following pages I will briefly sketch these four approaches.

(1) The Soviet marxist-leninist presentation of its own foreign policy strikes one by its almost total neglect of the socio-economic basis of this policy, limiting itself for the most part to the description of diplomatic procedures and principles of foreign policy, declarations and treaties, and only occasionally dealing with economic development and the political events of Soviet and international history. The presentation of its economic foundations is limited to a few lines or pages on the class character of foreign policy, without even touching on the influence upon foreign policy of the historic change in the class structure of the Soviet Union and the historically changing economic and social problems which have evolved since the end of the revolutionary period in its strict sense (ca. 1921). Foreign policy appears as the expression of a statically conceived class structure which has been maintained for decades and derives from a handful of constant "principles" of Soviet socialist foreign policy and from leninist "ideas". One does not even find the pretence of an analysis from the viewpoint of historical materialism; conclusions drawn from the history of ideas and diplomatic history dominate. Questions of social and class structure and of economic development are passed on to other specialists in the Soviet scientific enterprise.

One finds the following, for example, in a history of Soviet foreign policy, edited by leading Soviet experts:

> "In the course of hundreds and thousands of years, from that remote time when states first appeared upon the earth, both their domestic and their foreign policy — which regulates relations to other states — were determined by the interests of the dominant exploiting class. . . . No matter how the social and political forms changed, foreign policy was nevertheless at all times an instrument for the exploit-

ing minority. . . . This situation fundamentally changed with
the victory of the great socialist October revolution in Russia.
For the first time in the history of man, a completely new
foreign policy appeared, which did not serve the exploiters
but the working population — the class which had conquered
the government and represented the interests of the entire
labouring population. That was not possible without changes,
and in effect it changed the character of foreign policy, its
aims and problems, its sources of strength and its influence,
its means and methods. . . . The policy of any state whatsoever is ultimately determined by the character of its economic
and social order."[1]

The text emphasises the basic peculiarities of Soviet foreign
policy by contrasting it with capitalist-imperialist foreign policy:

"In capitalist society, which rests upon the private ownership of the means of production, upon the exploitation of
man by man, the strivings of the dominant class to maintain
its system of exploitation while expanding its sphere of
exploitation are the driving forces of foreign policy: markets,
the conquest of strategic positions and foreign territories,
and the enslavement of other peoples. The foreign policy of
capitalist countries is, because of their social nature, one of
expansion and aggression, of the preparation and execution
of wars of conquest, of the formation of military blocs and
the arms race."[2]

In a description of the nature of their own foreign policy, the
authors state:

"The foreign policy of the socialist countries is completely
different. In socialist society the social ownership of the
means of production dominates. Economic planning excludes
anarchy of production, crises and the struggle for markets.
Here there is no exploitation of man by man, no oppression
of nations. The driving force of socialist foreign policy is the
striving of the working class, which has the power in its
hands, to produce the most favourable conditions for con-
structing the new, most equitable and free society. . . .
Soviet foreign policy reflects the harmonious connection of

the international interests of the Soviet state and of the Soviet people with the international duties of the working class which has come to power. Soviet foreign policy combines patriotism and service to the interests of the Soviet homeland with internationalism."[3]

The Soviet marxist-leninist model postulates a hierarchy of the most important progressive agents of the socio-historical process. This hierarchy runs as follows: the international proletariat, the socialist community of states, and the Soviet people; and — within the latter — the working population, the working class, the Communist Party, the Central Committee of the Communist Party of the Soviet Union, the Politburo (which is however mentioned less often) and the General Secretary of the CPSU. The existence of basic conflicts of interest among these agents, representing different levels of abstraction, is denied. To be sure, the interests of these agents do not *a priori* rate as identical; they must first "combine" in a political process. Nevertheless, their fundamental "agreement" is constantly emphasised. D. G. Tomashevski, for example, writes:

"While in socialism, the interests of the dominant class — of the proletariat — and the interests of the nation as a whole agree, under the conditions of capitalism there exists a deep abyss between the interests of the nation and the interests of the dominant class."[4]

No official Soviet analysis of the socio-economic foundations of foreign policy takes up the question of when and where in Soviet society and Soviet history concrete differences of interest or even just differences of opinion and interpretation have manifested themselves — for instance, between the international proletariat and the Soviet people, between the working class and the peasants, between the workers and the party leadership.

To be sure, the theoretical philosophical literature of institutional Soviet marxism-leninism admits an explicit and open debate about the concept of interest.[5] It clearly affirms that there still exist both social and class differences and consequently specific contradictions of (non-fundamental, non antagonistic) interests.[6]

One of the leading representatives of Soviet philosophy, G. Y. Gleserman writes:

"Each question of political economy affects a number of specific interests and must be dealt with in relation to these interests. Let us take, for example, the distribution of investments among the individual branches of the economy. The securing of a rapid development for the most progressive branches of the economy corresponds to the interests of the people as a whole. Nevertheless, the redistribution of investment resources in favour of new branches can momentarily impair the interests of 'old' branches and be accompanied by contradictions. . . . Behind the figures indicating the tempo of development of the different branches stand men who are not only materially interested in the growth of the economy as a whole, but equally in the development of the branch in which they themselves are active."[7]

But how these interests conflict in reality, how the conflicts of interests are to be resolved and the interests harmonised, which positions emerge in the debate about the priority in investment decisions and in the distribution of the social product — all this remains hidden from the public. A harmony of interests and opinions is uncritically assumed at all stages of the hierarchy of progressive agents, from the international proletariat up to the General Secretary, but the claim to representation of the larger body by the smaller one (for example, the working population by the workers, or the working class by the party) is not based upon real processes of delegation or affinities of socio-economic interest. One overlooks the fact, too, that each form of mastery (and even that of the proletariat) implies slavery, that each form of leadership implies followers, that it implies masses of humans who are directed and managed by each form of directorship and management. The material for conflict that exists in this political division of labour is never mentioned. The contributions of institutional Soviet science are thus to a high degree unprofitable for the investigation of the socio-economic foundations of Soviet foreign policy.

(2) In its older form, that of the theory of totalitarianism, the bourgeois élite theory has essentially done nothing but to take

over the theoretical model of stalinist marxism-leninism and fitted it with opposing premises and an inverted set of values. It has simply reinterpreted the party's nominal claim to represent the working class and the Soviet people, the claim of the Central Committee to represent the party and that of the "leader" to represent the Central Committee, as a dictatorial and totalitarian assumption of power. In the attempt to focus in great detail upon personal constellations and decision-making processes, upon individual measures and shortcomings, there is a neglect of the general historical tendencies, the changes of socio-economic scenery against which the grisly drama of the struggle for power in the party leadership took place during the Stalin epoch. In the course of international détente — and of an actual break-up of the unity of the Soviet leadership — the bourgeois élite theory began to dismantle its model of Soviet society.[8] In place of monolithic unanimity, it suddenly discovered deep-seated conflicts of interest between the individual élite groups.[9] The organisational schemas of stratification sociology, directed towards the structure of its own society, have been transferred wholesale to Soviet society, with no consideration of the differences in productive relations.[10]

Generally speaking, these sociological investigations have no counterpart in the analysis of foreign policy, which traditionally only investigates governmental policy in connection with diplomatic or strategic objectives and with power struggles among the leadership.[11] Only perhaps in the case of a change of power do they go into the economic policies of the leading figures. In American literature on the subject one can find contributions dealing with the relation between the interests of élite factions and foreign policy, which nevertheless fail to actually demonstrate this relation.[12] In this context, the far-reaching changes in the socio-economic structure of Soviet society, since the October revolution, reflected in rapid industrialisation and urbanisation and in the accelerated growth of the working class and of the intelligentsia, receive no consideration. The question of to what extent a highly mechanised national economy, with a high division of labour and a relatively consolidated power structure, requires a different foreign policy from a society which is still in revolution and which has to contend with problems of economic subsistence and with the formation of a new political structure, has not been systematically discussed. Nevertheless, the numerous empirical investigations of economic development, of social relations as well as of foreign policy, are undoubtedly valuable for a more theoretically oriented presentation of foreign policy.

(3) Up to the present time there have been only isolated attempts to interpret Soviet foreign policy as springing from restored (or even initially maintained) capitalist productive relations in the Soviet Union. In the West, the most prominent analyses of "Soviet capitalism" or "neo-capitalism" limit themselves to domestic social and economic problems. Rita di Leo, for example, asserts:

> "To speak about the Soviet Union today means to speak about capitalism, about the continuing existence of the opposition between wage labour and capital."[13]

Bettelheim, on the other hand, sees tendencies towards a restoration of capitalist relations which he apparently believes to be not yet terminated.[14] Other authors emphasise the extra-territorial capitalist influence upon Soviet foreign policy without differentially analysing Soviet society itself; the Soviet Union appears as a self-enclosed social unit, harassed from without and compelled to adopt a conventional national foreign policy.[15] Chinese authors have also asserted the tendential restoration of capitalist relations in the Soviet Union. These latter arguments, however, rely apparently less upon an actual analysis of the relations of production than upon citations of ideological deviation from the marxist classics and upon the exposure of corruption, large differences in income, etc. — but without indicating the private expropriation of the surplus product as the dominant mode of production. The Soviet "bureaucratic bourgeoisie" is still designated as "a privileged social stratum" and thus not a "class", and Soviet "social imperialism" is distinguished from the usual capitalist "imperialism".[16]

(4) In contrast to the explanation dominant in East and West — that a society which has abolished private ownership of the means of production and nationalised the latter must be a socialist society with social ownership of the means of production — in the last decade, more and more theoretical attempts have gained ground which allow the possibility of a distinct social

formation, lying between the capitalist and the socialist-communist. Heidt and Mangeng focus strikingly upon the problem:

> "The discussion about the character of a new society frequently starts from the unexamined assumption that socialism would be the only alternative to capitalism, excluding the possibility of the revolutionary abolition of the capital relation in a non-socialist social formation. This position fails to recognise that the contradictions of capital relations can be abolished without a simultaneous elimination of the basis for alienated labour."[17]

To be sure, Heidt and Mangeng attack critiques of the non-socialist character of Soviet-type society which are based on "the difference between marxist ideas and existing reality",[18] but they themselves can only describe the "post-revolutionary" and "post-capitalist" society of the Soviet type as "non-socialist", because they hold the marxist notion of the abolition of alienated labour to be the sole valid notion of socialism.

The comparison between Soviet reality and the Marx-Engels conception of socialism (which was not simply a form of speculation about the future, interchangeable with any other, but rather an unchangeable component of the critique of capitalism) is and always has been the first step in a critical analysis of Soviet society.[19] Because of the political consequences which such an analysis can have, the marxist-leninist side rejects it:

> "When any concrete structure that we discover in socialist society is examined only to the extent that it diverges from structures which will exist in communist society, structural analysis tacitly turns into a critique of socialism: socialism then appears not as what it is — as the first phase of the communist social formation — but as kind of defective society [Mangelgesellschaft]."[20]

However correct the demand that one takes into account the historical state of development and the development tendencies of present-day social relations in the Eastern European countries, one cannot overlook the tendency of marxist-leninist social scientists to present and justify the existing state of socio-economic

relations in Eastern Europe, *cum grano salis,* as the only historically possible and objectively imperative one — and to denounce
any critique which goes beyond things as they are as "abstract"
and "a-historical".[21] Certainly the historical materialist analysis
of productive relations in Soviet society is still in its beginnings;
to derive the foreign policy of the Soviet Union from its socio-
economic relations is therefore, strictly speaking, not possible.

According to Ernest Mandel's interpretation, such an analysis
will not be able to make any progress in the foreseeable future,
since "we as yet lack the decisive historical material",[22] and the
new relations of production are still not completely developed.
Mandel supports this thesis by means of an analogy with transitional forms of productive relations — between the slave-holding
economy and feudalism (fourth to seventh centuries), and between
feudalism and capitalism (fifteenth to seventeenth centuries).
But this analogy, and its accompanying explanation for the un-
satisfying state of the historical materialist analysis of Soviet
society, fail to convince. Unlike earlier revolutions in the relations
of production, the new Soviet relations of production did not
grow up, so to speak, naturally over centuries in the bosom of the
old society, but resulted from an act of political volition (even if
it was not in fact a "conscious" one, with knowledge of the consequences). This process of radically transforming the relations
of production was essentially concluded in the 1930s — apart
from such relics as grey and black market production. All further
changes in productive relations have been up to now, and will
be for a long time to come, variations and mutations of the same
mode of production, which constantly brings forth new forms —
from nation to nation, from stage to stage.

With Charles Bettelheim one can, I think, really speak of a
special social formation "in transition between capitalism and
socialism",[23] although in my opinion the term "transitional
society" seems — without good cause — to ascribe instability and
a limited lifespan to such a society, while losing sight of the permanent transformation of the classic, in no way static or stable
modes of production.[24] As an alternative to distinguishing between
the "nationalisation" [*Verstaatlichung*] and the "socialisation"
[*Vergesellschaftung*][25] of the relations of production, the term
"statism" [*Etatismus*] as opposed to "socialism" seems provision-

ally useful.[26] One can designate a society with social ownership
of the means of production as a "bureaucratic society", after its
dominant social group.[27] Although a bureaucracy certainly existed
in earlier social formations (even a bourgeoisie came into being
long before bourgeois-capitalist society), its function was largely
instrumental, in the service of a social class. In Soviet society,
the bureaucracy became the dominant social group for the first
time — not without undergoing fundamental changes in the
make-up of its personnel, its social methods of recruitment and
above all its social function, because of the October revolution.
(Even the feudal guild bourgeoisie did not pass over unaltered
into the modern bourgeoisie.)

Problems in the analysis of Soviet society

Instead of embarking upon a detailed discussion of the various
attempts at analysing Soviet relations of production, I will now
more clearly define the problems which seem to me to be central
and to pose questions to which I have so far found only unsatisfactory answers.

Rosa Luxemburg, like Karl Marx before her,[28] emphasised that
the expansion of the capitalist mode of production, through
bloody conquest and the destruction of all "Chinese walls" by
means of cheap prices, had forged the world into *one* society,
bourgeois society:

> "There are not so many bourgeois societies, so many capita-
> lisms, as there are modern states and nations, but only one
> international society, one capitalism."[29]

Conflicts between bourgeois states therefore spring from conflicts *within* bourgeois society (not *between* several mutually
isolated societies) and consequently are subject to its laws. If
productive relations are changed fundamentally in one part of
international society, do there now exist two societies, a capitalist
and a non-capitalist one, which have the option (according to
their internal conditions alone) of either "peacefully coexisting"
or carrying on (hot or cold) war? Or is there a law which extends
to both social systems, which governs the relations of the two
state systems to one another?

Current analyses of the "world" market tacitly overlook the

fact that a third of mankind economically reproduces outside the capitalist sector of this world market. If one asserts that the capitalist sector of the world market also dominates the economy of socialist countries, imposing upon it a certain behaviour in foreign policy and even certain elements of social structure (e.g. through militarisation), is it a question of purely external "influence", a "supplementary" modification of the internal socio-economic processes? Doesn't such a thesis necessarily lead to abandoning any claim to methodological validity? After all, the relations between different "capitals" and capitalist states do not spring from expansive "driving forces" which are rooted within these bodies and isolated from one another, but from the capital relation which includes them. Is there also a social relation which comprehends both of the social and state systems?

Ernest Mandel quite rightly points out that it is not "competition" *between* the two social and state systems which determines the future of socialism, but class struggle resulting from social antagonisms *in* the individual countries.[30] But he does not ask whether there is a socio-historical law which covers the conflict and the competitive behaviour of the capitalist bourgeoisie and the Soviet bureaucracy as well as superseding the laws of the capitalist and *étatiste* social formation.

In Soviet society the means of production are state property. But what happens when one state enterprise "sells" something to another?[31] What is the difference between the transfer of property within a production unit and between production units? In the latter case there is no "change of ownership". Is there, then, a transfer of the "power of disposition"? What is the difference between "property" and the "power of disposition"?

The Soviet worker furnishes his labour power to the state enterprise for a remuneration; nevertheless, this labour power is not supposed to be a commodity.[32] Although the Soviet worker receives a wage, he is not supposed to be a wage employee. Soviet workers do not have control over the social surplus product — are they therefore "exploited"? (It is irrelevant simply to answer that the social services provided by the bureaucracy in the areas of medicine and education are relatively higher than under capitalism.) The bureaucrats dispose of the social products, but are not its owners.

In critiques of Soviet society, what is the exact meaning of the "separation" of workers from their means of production, the "isolation" of the bureaucracy from the producers, the "separation" of Soviet enterprises from one another? The control of the individual factory and of the individual factory management over the means of production is conditional; it is dependent upon changeable planning decisions from above, and other forms of state intervention. The manager is "politically" hired and fired; he is only the temporary and provisional commander of a certain part of the social product. To that extent he develops an interest in the reproduction and growth of what one could almost call a "state loan", which he can turn to his own profit under given conditions (among them being the well-known opportunities for circumventing planning directives). How does the competition between capital and wage earners differ from "socialist competition" between Soviet enterprises and workers?

There is a lot of evidence to indicate the existence of another phenomenon which is "intermediate" to private and social acquisition: i.e. temporary and conditional control, with perhaps a difference between the limited power of disposition of the individual bureaucrats and the larger, more comprehensive collective power of disposition of the bureaucracy as a whole. But that still does not tell us very much.

In any case, in my opinion, the notion that this "hybrid" character of Soviet productive relations, which are neither capitalist nor socialist and which still await closer description and explanation, also implies a historically "interim" or transitional character, can only be the result of wishful thinking — or anxiety. What real evidence is there to indicate that this as yet undetermined "interim" relation is socially and historically unstable and within a short period (i.e. within a few decades) will either have to turn into a capitalist or a socialist relation, as has been assumed since the time of the early marxist critics of Soviet society down to the present (Antonio Carlo, Charles Bettelheim, Ernest Mandel, Rita di Leo)? Just because Soviet productive relations are *theoretically* ambivalent (as long as we still think in terms of the categories of the critique of capitalism), this does not mean that they also necessarily possess a *historically* transitional character.

Consequences for the analysis of Soviet foreign policy

As long as we still lack a well developed theory of Soviet society, and ultimately of international society as a whole in the period of (peaceful or non-peaceful) coexistence of the two social systems, Soviet foreign policy cannot be derived from the socio-economic relations of the Soviet Union. All that is possible is to make a negative distinction between capitalist and Soviet (statist) foreign policy. One would have to demonstrate that in the previous history of Soviet foreign policy there has been no tendency to secure new markets for expansion just because of difficulties in capital realisation. At all events, the forms and methods of the policy of opening up foreign sources of raw materials would have to be more closely examined.[33]

The socio-economic constellation of interests in Soviet society, which one assumes to be different from that of bourgeois society, must be recognisable by means of empirical analyses of individual acts of foreign policy. And in fact Soviet foreign policy since the end of the revolutionary period (around 1923) has been conservative, dedicated to maintaining the international status quo. Soviet territorial expansion did not spring from internal problems and conflicts or pressures for expansion, but from military and strategic considerations of defence in the event of an offensive war against the Soviet Union — which did not, however, exclude the use of nationalistic formulas of legitimation (the liberation of "blood-related Ukrainian and White Russian brothers")[34] and of "historic legal claims" (the recovery of tsarist conquests, e.g. in East Asia).[35] The same can be said of the undeniable extension of strategic interests abroad by means of military support points (Cuba, the Mediterranean, the Indian Ocean), which does not, however, spring from the need to secure foreign markets and sources of raw materials.

How this international strategy of the Soviet Union relates to its social and economic structure has not been satisfactorily explained. In particular, the problem of national bureaucratic competition, exemplified most clearly between the Soviet Union and the People's Republic of China, cannot be understood by means of traditional interpretations of economic interests or of conflicts between the two systems.

To begin with, a differential analysis of foreign policy must pursue different paths which are not as yet connected with one another. It must (i) advance the theory of Soviet society (of bureaucratic society) and the analysis of non-capitalist productive relations in the Soviet Union and in other countries; (ii) continue the empirical analysis of Soviet social structure; (iii) present measures of foreign policy in terms of their historical changes and discontinuities; (iv) elaborate the always limited repertoire of nuances and policy variations of the organs of different ministries, social organisations and institutes, and thus of different sections of the bureaucracy, particularly when they become clear on the occasion of political upheavals and changes of power.

It is extremely difficult to discover the political nuances and variations between different social sectors. Thoroughgoing investigations, involving content analyses, show that there are no essential differences between the political comments of the military and civilian politicians. Previous studies at the Frankfurt Peace Research Institute show how difficult it is to detect differences between the foreign policies of different states, for example of the USSR and the German Democratic Republic.

The difficulty of uncovering the differences in which social and national dissimilarities in Eastern European society express themselves behind the monolithic wall of publications — newspapers, magazines, books and brochures, official documents — is certainly no proof that these differences do not exist. Behind the façade of public discussion of political problems, opinions and expressions of interest collide sharply. After the end of the conflict, they can emerge publicly in all their sharpness — usually upon the dismissal of party and government leaders, upon the exclusion of "deviating" (i.e. defeated) factions of the leadership (as in 1957), or — most openly — in social crises such as occurred in Czechoslovakia in 1968. Just before such events the political landscape still seems homogeneous; the factional struggles appear to break out without prior notice.

For the differential empirical analysis of political situations in "peaceful" times which are not marked by any spectacular social events, the following methods are available. (a) Even smaller political changes are not immediately visible in all the media; there are journalistic pacemakers which the other organs follow after several days or weeks. For example, we discovered that the new evaluation of the German SPD and FDP as "realistic" forces of the bourgeoisie just before the Bundestag election in 1969 was first expressed in the party and government organs, before it was to be found in the military ones. One can at least guess that the relatively positive evaluation of West Germany's *Ostpolitik* did not emanate from the Soviet Ministry of Defence. (b) Scientific and political controversies are usually not carried on in public; the selection of problems to be dealt with, the omission or reformulation of political stereotypes, and the varying degrees of sharpness or restraint of language in the presentation of one particular question, allow one to draw conclusions about political positions only with great caution. Speculation plays a large role, since one cannot decide on the basis of the material itself whether there is an actual difference of opinion or merely a "division of labour" in the journalistic strategy. (c) The conflict between bureaucracy and producers cannot be expressed directly in publications, since the bureaucrats possess a monopoly over the media. But from the content of the publication one can draw conclusions — once again not easily — about specific bureaucratic interests.

NOTES

1. B. N. Ponomarev, A. A. Gromyko, V. M. Khvostov (eds.), *Geschichte der sowjetischen Aussenpolitik 1917-1970* (Berlin [East] 1969 and 1971). In two parts: I, p. 12 ff. For the popular democracies, cf. II, p. 71.
2. Ibid., p. 13.
3. Ibid., p. 13-15.
4. D. G. Tomashevski, *Die Leninschen Ideen und die Internationalen Beziehungen der Gegenwart* (Berlin [East] 1973), p. 41.
5. The discussion was introduced by G. M. Gak, "Obshchestvennye i lichnye interesy i ikh sochetanie pri sotsialisme", in *Voprosy filosofii* 4 (1955), p. 17-28; cf. also A. S. Aïzikovich, "Vazhnaya sotsiologicheskaya problema", in *Voprosy filosofii* 11 (1965), p. 163-70; V.K. Zvol', "Sotsial'nye interesy vo vzaimodeistvii

ob'ektivnogo i sub'ektivnogo", in *Voprosy obshchestvennykh nauk* 9 (1972), p. 81-8.

6. Most authors speak only of *differences* of interest, less frequently of *contradictions* of interest and apparently never of *conflicts* of interest.

7. G. J. Gleserman, *Der Historische Materialismus und die Entwicklung der sozialistischen Gesellschaft* (Berlin [East] 1973), p. 140.

8. Hans Kaiser, "Vom 'Totalitarismus'- zum 'Mobilisierungs'-Modell", in *Neue Politische Literatur*, 18: 2 (1973), p. 141-69; Roger E. Kanet, "Neue Tendenzen in der amerikanischen Kommunismusforschung", in *Osteuropa*, 23: 4 (1973), p. 241-61.

9. Vernon V. Aspaturian, *Process and Power in Soviet Foreign Policy* (Boston 1971), p. 491 ff. I deal with the attempt to distinguish between a social coalition friendly to détente and one hostile to it in the essay, "The Role of the Armaments Complex in Soviet Society", in *Journal of Peace Research* 12: 3 (1975).

10. E.g., Karl-Eugen Wädekin, "Zur Sozialschichtung der Sowjetgesellschaft", in *Osteuropa* 15: 5 (1965), p. 321-9; David Lane, *The End of Inequality? Stratification under State Socialism* (Harmondsworth 1971).

11. Cf. most of the contribution in Dietrich Geyer (ed.), *Sowjetunion: Aussenpolitik 1917-1955* (Cologne 1972). An exception is Geyer's introductory chapter, which takes up theoretical questions relating to the mediation of social structure and foreign policy and explicitly points out the weakness in the thesis of a continuity in tsarist and Soviet foreign policy.

12. Cf. the contributions in Aspaturian.

13. Rita di Leo, *Die Arbeiter und das sowjetische System* (Munich 1973), p. 5.

14. Charles Bettelheim, *Economic Calculations and Forms of Property* (New York 1975).

15. Cf. Ursula Schmiederer, "Aspekte sowjetischer Aussenpolitik", in Peter W. Schulze (ed.), *Übergangsgesellschaft: Herrschaftsform und Praxis am Beispiel der Sowjetunion* (Frankfurt 1974), p. 151-200.

16. E.g., *Die Polemik über die Generallinie der internationalen kommunistischen Bewegung* (Berlin [West] 1970), in particular p. 463 ff.

17. Ulrich Heidt and Elisabeth Mangeng, "Parteivergesellschaftung. Uber den Zusammenhang von Transformationsprozeß und nachrevolutionären Gesellschaftsstrukturen in den nachkapitalistischen Ländern sowjetischen Typs", in Schulze, p. 90.

18. Ibid., p. 89.

19. See among others, Herbert Marcuse, *Soviet Marxism, a Critical Analysis* (New York 1958); Leo Kofler, *Stalinismus und Bürokratie* (Neuwied 1970); Oskar Negt, "Marxismus als Legitimationswissenschaft", in Negt, *Kontroversen über dialektischen und mechanistischen Materialismus* (Frankfurt 1974), p. 7-48; Bettelheim.

20. Manfred Lötsch, "Über die Entwicklung der Klassenstruktur und der Struktur der Arbeiterklasse beim Aufbau der entwickelten sozialistischen Gesellschaft", in M. Lötsch and M. Meyer, *Zur Sozialstruktur der sozialistischen Gesellschaft* (Berlin [East] 1974), p. 46.

21. E.g. Gleserman, p. 21.

22. Ernest Mandel, "Ten Theses on the Social and Economic Laws Governing the Society Transitional Between Capitalism and Socialism", in *Critique* 3 (1974), p. 7.

23. Bettelheim.

24. For additional arguments against the designation "transitional society", cf. Egbert Jahn, *Kommunismus — und was dann?* (Reinbek 1974), p. 81 ff.

25. Cf. Bettelheim.

26. Since the term "state" always implies rule by a minority — except in a brief transitional period to a socialist/communist society — the objection of Heidt and Mangeng to the expression "statism" (ibid., p. 109) is not convincing.

27. For the reasons which make the designation "class" seem inappropriate for the Soviet bureaucracy, see Mandel, p. 16 ff. and Jahn, p. 88 ff. For counter arguments, see Bettelheim and Antonio Carlo.

28. Karl Marx and Friedrich Engels, XIX Werke (Berlin [East] 1973), p. 28.

29. Rosa Luxemburg, *Internationalismus und Klassenkampf. Die polnischen Schriften* (Neuwied 1971), p. 292 ff.

30. Mandel, "Wettkampf der Systeme", in E. Krippendorf, ed., *Probleme der internationalen Beziehungen* (Frankfurt 1972), p. 219.

31. Current Soviet textbooks do not go into this question; cf. e.g. A. F. Rumyantsev *et al.* (eds.), *Politische Ökonomie des Sozialismus* (Frankfurt 1973), p. 163.

32. Ibid., p. 164.

33. Cf. e.g. Karl Wohlmuth, "Sozialistische Länder" und "Dritte Welt", in B. Tibi and V. Brandes (eds.), *Handbuch 2. Unteren-*

twicklung (Frankfurt 1975), p. 271-300.
34. Cf. Geyer, p. 84.
35. Ponomarev et al., vol. 2, p. 147.

2

Revolutionary foreign policy in a capitalist environment

EKKEHART KRIPPENDORFF

In a historical perspective the problem of "revolutionary" foreign policy does not appear for the first time in the year 1917: without doing violence to history, one can already find structural parallels in the Cromwellian revolution. Its possible socio-political consequences were, for example, clearly perceived by the political class in France which had just succeeded in restabilising state and society after a bloody, still smouldering civil war. Cromwellian foreign policy used the French fear of civil war as one of its means for neutralising France in relation to English plans for expansion abroad. What one can see here in a merely nascent phase became an open problem with the outbreak of the French revolution: the *anciens régimes* had to reverse it for the sake of their own self-preservation, since the appeal of the self-confident French bourgeoisie subverted the legitimacy of the dominant classes and princely houses of Europe. And inversely: the revolutionary appeal of the French bourgeoisie to class solidarity from the European middle class was aimed at securing the fruits of its own revolutionary struggles, and this was a weapon in the French republic's fight for survival in a hostile environment. The downfall of the European states before the onslaught of the Napoleonic armies was less a military-strategic event than a socio-political one — and not only a socio-political one. Napoleon, or rather French continental policy, was the midwife for the manufacturing and industrial bourgeoisie in Central Europe and at the same time drew its socio-economic substance from this class: the creation of a European market for the capitalist mode of production.

The structural affinity implied here between the foreign policy of the revolutionary French middle class in an absolutist-

monarchical environment and that of the revolutionary foreign
policy of the first proletarian state in a capitalist environment after
1917 could provide important information for determining the
military and political aspects of foreign policy: the role of sub-
versive, demoralising propaganda directed at enemy armies; the
undermining of the legitimacy of conservative régimes; the
systematic violation of diplomatic rules; revolutionary warfare,
etc. But interpreted too broadly, such a parallel loses sight of one
important difference: among other things, the proletarian revolution differs fundamentally from the bourgeois revolution in that
the latter brings to political power a class already in possession of
the means of production, one which has already become the
leading class economically and socially and which by means of the
bourgeois revolution "merely" destroys the political structures
which hinder its further development. The working class, on the
other hand, however strong it is in numbers and in political
organisation (in its class consciousness), does not draw its strength
from control over the means of production: it must not only
occupy the political and administrative command posts, it must
simultaneously, and not last of all, take over the economic means
of social reproduction; it must develop a new mode of production
in the process of destroying the capitalist mode of production,
which took centuries to mature.

As a social formation, the middle class grew up slowly but
surely within feudal society on the basis of its superior mode of
production, promoting itself to the leading class — one which
could effectively lay claim to ideological, social and finally political
leadership. The working class likewise arose within a social
order which blocked its own self-realisation, its full emancipation;
but its basis was and is not a new mode of production in competition with the capitalist one — one which would more effectively
develop the productive forces (notwithstanding arguments to that
effect, for example, by Blanquists) — but a massive negation of
the capitalist mode of production and the transformation of it
after the political revolution.

The question of whether the revolutionary destruction of
Russia's capitalist economic order, which had undergone a rapid
and powerful development since the turn of the century, was
"correct" or historically justified (Bolsheviks versus Mensheviks),

is a historical one in the negative sense of the term. No doubt the Bolsheviks not only assumed that the working class in Western Europe would follow the "signal" set off in Russia, but that they also had every reason — in view of the disintegration of Western European societies in the wake of the war, and the historic strength of the Western European working-class movement — to count on such a further development of the revolutionary process and to employ this as a real factor in legitimising the revolutionary upheaval. One could not foresee that these expectations would remain unfulfilled — the risk of failure is, by definition, included in every revolution. Once, however, the capitalist social order in Russia had been politically destroyed, and once this destruction remained an isolated event, the question now arose as to the possibility of developing a non-capitalist mode of production under conditions of a world market dominated and shaped by the capitalist mode of production. As is well known, the problem was especially acute for a Russia that was comparatively backward and heavily affected by war, and the solutions became secondary to the primary problem of the sheer survival of Soviet power.

The first proletarian revolution could only survive under three conditions. First by militarily defending itself against the "White" armies during the civil war, which were partly directed from without, and against foreign intervention. Secondly, by creating for itself — in contrast to Lenin's original revolutionary concept of superseding the bourgeois state with new institutions (the soviets) — a strong government apparatus; this latter was the result of an externally imposed compulsion to survive, and was itself a complicated process of improvisation which grew up in an undirected, reactive and organic fashion.[1] And thirdly, by making its economy capable of functioning as quickly as possible and by reducing the enormous lead which European capitalist industrial states had over it in the development of productive forces. These three conditions could also be described as forming a temporal sequence: an immediate or short-range goal, military survival; a middle-range one, governmental-political stabilisation (not least by means of organisation and repressive force); and in the long term, the comprehensive development of production as the precondition for the possibility of socialism and communism, of the universal fulfilment of all needs. For the last of these goals the central problem was — and is — the fact that socialist possibilities are conditioned by a capitalist dominated world market; nevertheless, socialist production is oriented to the development of society as a whole in a comprehensive sense, unlike capitalist production, which on the contrary is oriented to quantitive economic growth (the profitable valorisation of capital).

But there is still another goal (balanced development of society as a whole instead of sectoral economic growth) that seems to be unattainable under conditions of global market competition with the capitalist mode of production. Let us illustrate the problem by taking a look at Tanzania's socialist experiment. In 1967, President Nyerere expounded the Arusha Declaration in the following words:

> "Inherent in the Arusha Declaration, therefore, is the rejection of the concept of national grandeur as distinct from the well-being of its citizens, and a rejection too, of material wealth for its own sake. It is a commitment to the belief that there are more important things in life than the amassing of riches, and that if the pursuit of wealth clashes with things like human dignity and social equality then the latter will be given priority. . . . With our present level of economic activity, and our present poverty, this may seem to be an academic point; but in reality it is very fundamental. So it means that there are certain things which we shall refuse to do or accept, whether as individuals or a nation, even if the result of them would give a surge forward in our economic development."[2]

Tanzania might be capable of putting such a programme into socio-political practice (although recent signs of crisis give reason for scepticism); but for a Soviet Union fighting for its existence, it was inevitable that it should orient its priorities towards survival. It therefore had to practice sectorally forced economic growth, especially in those areas in which it was most vulnerable to the capitalist economies — and thus in areas whose law of economic growth was and is inevitably oriented not to society as a whole but to what is most profitable.

The "practical disappearance of Russia from the stage of the

international economy"[3] which took place during the 1920s does
not seem to have been the result of a politico-economic strategy
on the part of the Soviet leadership, but rather to have depended
upon the radical decline of Soviet production, the refusal of most
capitalist countries to establish trade and the impossibility of
obtaining loans. In any case, the early Bolshevik leaders did not
plan to disentangle Soviet Russia from the capitalist world market
but to integrate it as far as possible, for which purpose they saw
Russia's raw materials as a trump-card in winning concessions. In
early 1921, Rykov believed:

> "The quantity of raw materials which Western Europe
> [traditionally] received from Russia is so great that without
> these materials, without Soviet Russia's participation in the
> restoration of the European economy, the restoration . . .
> will be impossible."[4]

Lenin agreed:

> "For the world economy to be restored, Russian raw materials
> must be utilised. You cannot get along without them — that
> is economically true. It is admitted even by . . . a student of
> economics who regards things from a purely bourgeois
> standpoint. That man is Keynes."[5]

Trotsky was initially sceptical about this assumption of a
readiness on the part of capitalist countries to assist socialist
Russia, and in 1920 wanted to "substitute labour for [the
missing] capital"[6], in which Lenin (in February 1920) partially
supported him: the economy must be reconstructed "by military
methods, with absolute ruthlessness and by the suppression of
all other interests."[7] Again, Trotsky said quite clearly (in January
1920):

> "Possibly we will succeed in importing some locomotives
> from America . . . but we must not pin our hopes on them.
> We must speak of what we can do in the country during an
> epoch of nearly total blockade."[8]

Lenin, Rykov and the others nevertheless emphasised the need
to import technology both by means of exporting raw materials
and by guaranteeing concessions to capitalist enterprises in Soviet

Russia. NEP and the politico-military stabilisation seemed to justify this tactic. In 1925, Trotsky said:

> "We ourselves have been extremely cautious, one might even say too cautious, with respect to concessions agreements. We were afraid that the introduction of foreign capital would undermine the still weak foundations of socialist industry. . . . We are still very backward in a technical sense. We are interested in using every possible means to accelerate our technical progress. Concessions are one way to do this. Despite our economic consolidation, or more precisely, because of our economic consolidation, we are now more inclined than a few years ago to pay foreign capitalists significant sums for . . . their participation in the development of our productive forces."[9]

Capitalism became the creditor of socialism, it financed its own opponent (this was interpreted as "the dialectic of historical development") — the problem was to stimulate "the transfer to our country of foreign plant, foreign productive formulae, and the financing of our economy by the resources of world capitalist savings".[10]

The tone of triumph familiar to us from present day Soviet pronouncements of the Brezhnevian variety, namely that the blockade policy of the cold war has failed and that the crisis-torn capitalist countries must now trade with the economically stable Soviet Union in spite of themselves — for mutual advantage, of course — one can find almost word for word in Trotsky in 1925:

> "However, with the rapid growth of exports and imports the position has radically changed. We are becoming a part, a highly individual but nevertheless component part of the world market."[11]

In 1926 he projected the integration of the Soviet Union with Western Europe as a means of industrialisation, once again on the basis of exchanging raw materials against technology and certainly before, or independently of, revolution in the West:

> "The Kursk deposits of magnetic iron, the Ural potassium deposits, and all our gigantic resources in general demand the application of international savings and world technology."[12]

Today, Brezhnev says the same thing, word for word. He would not even contest Trotsky's thesis of 1927:

> "Other conditions being equal foreign capital must be attracted to those branches of industry which show the greatest backwardness . . . by comparison with the corresponding branches of world industry."[13]

Today, this chiefly means the motor industry.

Without examining the extent to which reality contradicted the wishes and declarations of intent, what we must always remember about Soviet economic strategies is that they must be viewed against the background of the theoretically well-founded (and, in the end, practically verified) hypothesis of the "unavoidability" or "probability" of intercapitalist wars, of wars into which the Soviet Union would necessarily be drawn if it were not to become their chosen victim. The diversification of Soviet foreign trade and the corresponding diversification of Soviet foreign policy appear either as a means of preventing war (maximal) or as a means of retarding it (minimal). Once again, Trotsky in 1925:

> "The more multiform our international relations, the more difficult it will be . . . for our possible enemies to break them. And . . . even if (war or blockade) . . . were to come about, we should still be much stronger than we would have been under a 'self-sufficient' and consequently belated development."[14]

Its envisaged role as an integral component of the world market thus included for the Soviet Union the (temporary) subordination of global social development to the law of sectoral economic growth. Within a specific period, the conditions imposed by the capitalist world market and by the more progressive or more advanced technology of the capitalist competitors would determine which sectors these were to be — heavy industry, armaments, space technology, chemistry etc. *After* the proletarian revolution on a world scale, Bukharin asserted in 1927,

> "Our problem will be that of developing production and of rationalising it in such a way that we can take account of the most favourable geographical, climatic, logistic, technical and other conditions."

But it would be premature under the conditions of a world market dominated by capitalism:

> "But matters do not stand that way now. Now the world economy, unfortunately, is not under the dictatorship of the proletariat. . . . We are struggling and we must struggle to become more independent of this world capitalist economy. And when we hear . . . that our 'national limitation' lies in this (belief) we can only chuckle. Our independence is independence of a class type, an independence of the capitalist states."[15]

The class content thus appears as the *differentia specifica* between the bourgeois and proletarian state, as the necessary foundation of the latter's historical novelty. The bourgeois state protected the capitalist mode of production — which had grown up in the womb of feudal society and whose class had now attained political power — by sanctioning, among other things, private ownership of the means of production. The proletarian state, however, needs qualified cadres, competent administrators and ideologues who will secure and legitimise its authority; it must first create, train and educate its personnel and act as a motor force implementing a new socialist mode of production — with the result that its antagonist, the bourgeoisie (which had "originally" become the dominant class by its control of the means of production), describes it as a "totalitarian state". Nonetheless, one could say that by a conscious and systematic absorption of techniques of production whose specific origin and function within the context of the capitalist mode of production was overlooked, forms of production which are today interchangeable with those of the capitalist mode of production sneaked in through the backdoor of the proletarian-ruled state forms of production, which are in fact even more backward, "more exploitative" than are those of capitalism in the 1970s. The Fiat management, for example, has favourably compared the labour discipline of Soviet workers in Togliattigrad with that of its own Italian working class. One must, however, always bear in mind the enormous external pressures which the Soviet Union had to withstand; China, by contrast, had the chance not only to learn from the negative experiences of the Soviet example, but also to pursue its own development for a critical decade under the protection of the by then powerful Soviet Union:

> "The absorption of highly developed techniques of production from capitalist countries had necessarily to lead to the absorption of capitalist forms of the division of labour and corresponding systems for materially stimulating workers (piecework, taylorism). The low degree of adaptability of the labour force to these forms demanded a quasi-military form of authoritarian labour discipline . . . with the inevitable result (the inevitability came from the organisation of production) of an expansion in the functions of the central planning bureaucracy and of executive management. The concentration of means for the provision of a comprehensive, technically highly developed apparatus for the means of production, at the expense of mass consumption, 'led' necessarily to the growth of a strong state apparatus."[16]

And this state apparatus in turn pursued a foreign policy of *raison d'état* oriented to its own self-preservation which hardly differed in form from that of the governmentally determined foreign policy of the capitalist societies. A definition of Soviet foreign policy such as that offered by Foreign Minister Gromyko in the 28 June 1968 issue of *Pravda* could have come from any foreign minister of any country whatsoever:

> "Our foreign policy is and will continue to be characterised by resoluteness in defending the state interests of the Soviet people, in safeguarding the inviolability of our land frontiers, maritime coasts and air space, and in protecting the dignity of the Soviet flag and the rights and security of Soviet citizens."[17]

Is it just in its *form* that the governmentally determined foreign policy of the Soviet "transitional society" increasingly approximates to that of capitalist industrial nations, or is it also in its *content*, as the maoist thesis asserts? Is the superpower conflict between the USA and the USSR an intercapitalist one? Has the subordination of the goal of global social development to the efficient economic growth of certain key sectors with the help of capitalist production techniques and, more recently, the further opening up of the Soviet economy to Western capital (which nonetheless cannot acquire means of production), led to a restoration of capitalism in the Soviet Union? Or is that the logical consequence of such a strategy of opening up? I am by and large convinced by Mandel's argument,[18] according to which the competition of capitals and free saleability of the means of production are lacking in the Soviet Union and one cannot therefore speak even of an inchoate restoration of capitalism. On the other hand, even Mandel takes into consideration the following:

> "Without doubt there are forces within the bureaucracy which objectively press in the direction of a restoration of capitalism. The demand that more powers be given to the enterprise directors; the demand for the power to dismiss workers; the demand in the context of Liberman reforms for the power to 'negotiate' 'free prices' for raw materials and manufactured goods; all these tendencies objectively correspond to a pressure towards putting the law of value back into command."[19]

And it is exactly this tendency, which at least some of the Western strategies for closer co-operation with the Soviet Union aim at as a welcome by-product of mutual enterprise — the tendency towards direct contact at plant level, the introduction of capitalist know-how, labour-saving techniques etc. — which leads to a weakening of central planning, to the setting off of an inflationary spiral and, last but not least, to unemployment. In 1965, de Sola Pool speculated:

> "Around 1980, there will be a major political crisis in the Soviet Union, marked by large-scale strikes, the publication of dissident periodicals, a temporary disruption of central control over some regions, and an open clash between the major sectors of the bureaucracy over questions of military policy and consumer goods. This will stop just short of revolution, though it will result in the effectual abolition of the Communist Party or its splitting up into more than one organisation, the abolition of the kolkhoz, and so forth. During these events, the Soviet hold over Eastern Europe will be completely broken."[20]

If this projection, which is exaggerated by wishful thinking, is essentially correct — that is, if the Soviet Union and its Eastern European economic associates or states are in fact headed for a period of externally induced social conflict, as a result of its competitive integration within the capitalist world market and the disparities of efficiency which this mode of producton produces — we would then have a fairly plausible "internal political" explanation for the Soviet diplomatic policy of securing its territorial integrity by means of the Helsinki agreement: the strategy of securing the political and military levels so that the expected socio-political conflict, both within the Soviet Union and the Eastern European states as well as between them, cannot be exploited by Western "intervention" of any kind whatsoever. The "deportation" of undesirable individuals would find its logic in all this, as well as the supposed "liberalisation" of emigration policies for Soviet Jews.

But Soviet foreign policy under capitalist world market conditions does not exhaust itself in the policy of peaceful coexistence, which is far more complex than its conceptual simplicity would apparently indicate. The Soviet Union has found itself compelled to take sides in the inter-imperialist conflicts of the 1970s. Without underestimating the significance of the offer and the practical possibilities of bilateral relations of co-operation with Western Europe and Japan, the Soviet Union seems to aim strategically at the United States, with a desire to help the latter strengthen its weakened position in relation to its imperialist competitors, to restore the American leading role in the capitalist "camp". According to Foreign Minister Gromyko, the United States has "discovered that in pursuing a policy of confrontation with the Soviet Union, it was only weakening its own position relative to other capitalist countries,"[21] which leads to the logical conclusion that the "radical improvement" in Soviet-American relations will lead to the re-establishment of the leading position of the US. To the other capitalist countries, the Soviet Union offers itself or its markets as an escape hatch from the crises caused by intercapitalist competition, to West German capital[22] as well as to threatened Italian industry.[23]

At all events, the Soviet Union is not pleased at the prospect of a severe crisis within the capitalist world market, with its unforeseeable potential for political and military conflict. The semi-official *Textbook of Political Economy* offers the following general formulation:

> "Trade with socialist states is advantageous even for capitalist countries and becomes increasingly more attractive to them, owing to the success of the former countries in science and technology. The socialist countries offer the capitalist entrepreneur a very receptive market, something which is very important for the latter owing to aggravated problems with marketing."[24]

For their part, at least some American economic leaders have unmistakeably declared that improved economic or trade relations with the Soviet Union could contribute to diminishing or mitigating an American recession.[25] On the other hand, however, the capitalist world market does not only consist of metropolises but also of so-called "peripheries", which have a potential for conflict that is not only unusually larger but manifests itself more quickly, and towards which the Soviet Union sees itself compelled to take a position.

The Soviet Union's misinterpretation of the anti-capitalist possibilities and potential of the third world emerged dramatically for the first time in its underestimation of the Chinese Communist Party, and then in the economic burden which Cuba became on the Soviet Union (around 1,500,000 dollars per day).[26] The overestimation of revolutionary potential, on the other hand, and the disappointed expectations from national liberation and similar movements in the early 1960s, first appeared in black Africa, where not one of seven promising conflict situations developed in the direction of a pro-Soviet change of power.[27] The tried and tested policy of rapid economic growth within the capitalist world market has at this stage led to an openly "counter-revolutionary" strategy or at least to one which is sceptical of revolution in the third world; it is oriented towards reciprocal economic advantage, rather than primarily towards strengthening anti-capitalist forces and movements. With respect to the Arab states, for example, the Soviet Union supports the growth of a "state capitalist" bureaucracy:

"Its relations with the 'progressive' Arab countries have tended to encourage the establishment of such a system, to the detriment of local communist parties and other opposition forces, both for the protection of Soviet investment and, in the longer term, for the channelling of Soviet political influence."[28]

Increasingly, foreign aid is seen as an alternative to domestic investment:

"It would be cheaper for the USSR to import certain goods and materials than to produce them at home. Similarly . . . the East European states [are to] replace some of the raw materials they obtained from the Soviet Union by imports from Africa and the Middle East."[29]

This would afford the Soviet Union greater trade manoeuvrability in relation to the USA, Western Europe and Japan. Together with this stabilisation strategy on the capitalist periphery, a more acute sense of sociological differentiation in analysing third world countries, observable since the middle of the 1960s, resulted in the USSR indirectly admitting that under certain conditions, capitalist help from abroad and technical industrial expertise would have a positive effect in overcoming underdevelopment, while the premature and radical nationalisation of foreign firms would on the contrary have the negative and damaging effect of frightening off further capitalist investments.[30] Although the rhetoric of Soviet third world diplomacy is ambivalent, and although officially (for example, in the form of approval for the declarations of certain Latin American communist parties) armed struggle has not ben rejected under "objective conditions", the dominant concern — not least because of the continuing Cuban experience — is for the economic burden, not to mention the military one, involved in a peripheral country successfully escaping from the imperialist chain. In spite of all the warm words which Brezhnev had for Chile, there was no hint of an "international obligation" to support Chile, in contrast to the concern which was displayed for Czechoslovakia.[31]

But although tactically counterrevolutionary, Soviet foreign policy still retains an objectively revolutionary element, to the extent that under conditions of a competition between systems it is actually compelled to collaborate with social groups and political classes which wish to free themselves from the dominance of American capitalism and imperialism. It is only in exceptional cases that these groups and classes aim explicitly at socialist revolution, but in order to rally support for their anti-imperialist strategy, they have to rely upon certain social forces which must be seen as revolutionary in the sense that they seek to reshape productive relations in a socialist direction.

NOTES

1. Walter Pietsch, *Revolution und Staat: Institutionen als Träger der Macht in Sowjetrußland 1917-1922* (Cologne 1969); Dietrich Geyer, *Die Russische Revolution* (Stuttgart 1968), p. 118 f.
2. Robin Jenkins, *Exploitation: the World Power Structure and the Inequality of Nations* (London 1970), p. 41.
3. W. Arthur Lewis, *Economic Survey 1919-1939* (London 1949), p. 32.
4. Richard B. Day, *Leon Trotsky and the Politics of Economic Isolation* (Cambridge, Mass. 1973), p. 51.
5. Ibid.
6. Ibid., p. 25.
7. Ibid., p. 24 f.
8. Ibid., p. 26.
9. Ibid., p. 132.
10. Ibid., p. 133.
11. Ibid., p. 134.
12. Ibid., p. 171.
13. Ibid.
14. Ibid., p. 135.
15. Ibid., p. 168.
16. Wolf Rosenbaum, "Die Funktion von Staat und Recht in der Ubergangsgesellschaft", in Peter Hennicke (ed.), *Probleme des Sozialismus und der Ubergangsgesellschaften* (Frankfurt 1973), p. 65.
17. Cited after W. W. Kulski, *The Soviet Union in World Affairs. A Documented Analysis 1964-1972* (Syracuse 1973), p. 27.

18. Ernest Mandel, "Ten Theses on the Social and Economic Laws Governing the Society Transitional Between Capitalism and Socialism", in *Critique* 3 (1974), p. 5-21.
19. Ibid., p. 18.
20. I. de Sola Pool, "The International System in the Next Half Century", in *Toward the Year 2000*, D. Bell (ed.) (Boston 1968), p. 321, note 1; cited in J. Wilczynski, *Socialist Economic Development and Reforms: from Extensive to Intensive Growth and Central Planning in the USSR, Eastern Europe and Yugoslavia* (New York 1972), p. 327.
21. *International Affairs* 10 (1973), p. 69.
22. Ibid., p. 74 ff.
23. Ibid., no. 7, p. 27.
24. From Volkhard Brandes, *Die Krise des Imperialismus* (Frankfurt 1973), p. 82.
25. Wilczynski, ibid., p. 316.
26. *Neue Züricher Zeitung*, 1 August 1971.
27. Morton Schwartz, "The USSR and Leftist Régimes in Less-Developed Countries", in *Survey* 2 (1973), p. 209-44.
28. Robin Buss, "Wary Partners: the Soviet Union and Arab Socialism", in *Adelphi Papers* 73 (London 1973), p. 1.
29. Elizabeth K. Valkenier, "Soviet Economic Relations with the Developing Nations", in Roger E. Kanet (ed.), *The Soviet Union and the Developing Nations* (Baltimore 1974), p. 219.
30. Ibid., p. 228; Valkenier, "Recent Trends in Soviet Research on the Developing Countries", in Raymond W. Duncan (ed.), *Soviet Policy in Developing Countries* (Waltham, Mass. 1970), p. 305 ff.
31. Ronald R. Pope, "Soviet Foreign Policy Toward Latin America", in *World Affairs* 2 (1972), p. 163.

3

The relation between détente and Soviet economic reforms

HILLEL TICKTIN

The first thesis of this paper is that the origins of the economic reforms and détente are the same but that the failure of the economic reforms propelled the USSR on to a line of policy which involved increased co-operation with the West. Secondly the economic reforms themselves required an increasing degree of contacts in different ways with the West and thirdly this co-operation has in fact taken the form of increasing concessions and dependence on the most advanced capitalist powers, which has in turn demanded a move to further reform.

It is important to understand the reasons for the economic reforms before coming to grips with the relationship between them and foreign policy. There are some persons, mainly apologists or alternatively those most interested in attacking the basis of planning of any type, who are of the view that the USSR has consistently maintained a centrally planned economy and indeed society from 1929 onwards. Its modern problems arise from the unsuitability of applying a previous model to its contemporary situation. The problem with this view is that it has no class content or expressed in different terms it fails to observe the social origins of the Soviet economy. Marxists accustomed to demonstrating the social nature of economic categories often refuse to analyse these same economic categories when applied to the USSR. It is therefore necessary to begin the discussion with some reference to the nature of the economic laws operating in the USSR and their socio-economic content. The reasons for the economic reforms then follow from the contradictions in the Soviet economy.

Historical roots of the economic problems

Michael Ellmann has already described in his works some of the problems to which the Soviet élite were reacting.[1] The different symptoms, however, can be reduced to an insufficiency in supply of consumer goods, food in particular, low quality of all types of goods and thirdly, the omnipresent problems of waste. These three aspects of the Soviet economy have in fact been present in one form or another since the onset of industrialisation and collectivisation and indeed, in a different form and order of importance, before it. Preobrazhensky expressed the contradiction the Bolsheviks found themselves in as follows: "In the period of preliminary accumulation the socialist form . . . has not yet developed all its advantages, but it has lost some of the advantages of a capitalist economy".[2] He essentially argues that the Soviet economy is necessarily inefficient. The state sector cannot employ the modes of exploitation used by the private sector such as overtime, unemployment and one could add excessive differentiation in income, speed-up on the production line, avoidance of safety and health regulations and even pollution laws. On the other hand, the socialist or public sector lacked both the "material prerequisites for reconstructing its technical bases and the necessary prerequisites of socialist culture and socialist education of the working proletariat".[3] In the twenties, therefore, the problem was twofold: the technical one of obtaining modern machinery, and the social one of the education and re-education of the working-class. This latter precondition must really be linked with his view that the driving force of the economy was the pressure of the working class.[4] He even goes so far as to speak of what amounts to industrial sabotage as a means of pressure. A period of preliminary socialist accumulation was, therefore, required before the advantages of socialism could show themselves in terms of efficient, high-technology and high-quality production. In fact, both Marx and Lenin, in the *Critique of the Gotha Programme* and *State and Revolution,* make a point very close to this when they speak of the first phase of communist society being one in which the attitude to work is changed from compulsion to need. Effectively what Preobrazhensky has done is to draw out the implications of this view for the transition period occurring in a society which is not the most advanced capitalist nation in the world economy. Whereas for Marx and Lenin it is reward according to ability which will serve as an incentive to the worker, together with his increasingly direct identification with the aims of the society, for Preobrazhensky the situation is much more complex. The absence of democratic means of identification with the society requires indirect forms of pressure. The worker is subjected to the needs of accumulation and consequently receives less than he would in a socialist society and he is, therefore, subject still to payment for his labour power as a commodity. It would appear as if the incentives are some fusion between market-capitalist incentives and what are now called moral incentives. In fact he states that the incentives to be employed are not yet clear. What he does make abundantly clear is their contradictory nature.

It is, of course, the whole question of economic incentives that is at the heart of the economic reforms and it is important to note that the problem posed right at the beginning of the régime has still not been resolved. In fact I would argue that the contradiction noted by Preobrazhensky has continued to the present day, but in a mutated form. The insoluble contradiction between plan and market, wholly insoluble in one country as Preobrazhensky observed, was removed in that form by the consolidation of power by the bureaucracy. It constituted itself as a new élite which held the means of administration in its own hands and effectively destroyed all opposition forces, either directly through physical liquidation or indirectly through a process of atomisation so thorough and so deep that it made the régime unique in its power over the population. The market forces of the peasantry and urban private sector had operated in conjunction with this bureaucracy for some time. In fact the latter had come to include in its ranks both old bourgeois specialists, non-specialists who simply possessed the elementary skills required in a civil ervice leading an illiterate population, and Bolsheviks who had become corrupted by the interplay with the market in an atmosphere of scarcity. This was noted by the party as early as 1920, when a debate was held around the question of the degeneration of the party.[5] The effect by 1929 was to turn the party apparatus into a group which wished to perpetuate the hierarchy in production, the difference in rewards and so the incentive system inherent in a market. On the other hand they held their own positions outside the market and possessed neither the skills nor the historical possibility to revert to the market itself. Historically the Whites had just been defeated, and it might not have been so easy to fend them off in a return to capitalism. More important, however, was the fact that their positions were not stable, being under challenge from left and right; the only method of consolidation was to find a way which would both destroy the social bases of the oppositions and expand the basis of their own power. This was done through the introduction of a police state which terrorised the countryside and so broke its political importance forever, at the same time as industrialisation at an extreme rate recruited a wholly raw and atomised working class, only to glad to escape from the horrors of the countryside. The physical apparatus of the base of their rule was vastly expanded, both through the expansion of the centralised functions of the state and administration as well as the not inconsiderable growth of state enterprises.

It is important to realise that the socio-economic nature of what in fact occurred was a supersession of the market, in the sense that market methods were employed (as in the extreme introduction of piece-rates and wide differences in incomes, with one-man management and a hierarchical structure) without the market itself existing. The actual levers used to obtain the priorities set were of a market type, for example low prices for producer goods, higher wages for producer goods workers and lower wages for light industry. The consequences of this situation were unforeseen but predictable. It became inevitable that a factory director would prefer to employ a man to a woman, since he has fewer days off because of children, and women came to occupy the least well-paid and prestigious occupations in the economy. The point is that this situation has come about spontaneously, given the market-type structure. Again it is entirely to be expected that the unproductive occupations would be both less favoured and less well paid. The pay of doctors, teachers, clerks and distributive workers is notorious. In other words, the spontaneous tendencies of the economy tend to move in a market direction.

On the other hand, the organisational nature of the industrial structure both removed any real market and existed in a permanent tension with the market-like tendencies. It was the "plan" which imposed the need to accumulate, though the over-accumulation which followed was uncontrollable. The result has been that the "planning" has been seldom successful except in the broadest terms, and then only when there has been concentration on particular sectors. In the early years it was the extraction of the absolute surplus from the working class which built industry. While the camps played no small economic role, in a sense the whole of the USSR was a camp in which it was force or the threat of force which provided the negative incentive to the positive one of market-type rewards. A series of new structures came into existence, of which force was only one of the "planned elements". It has never been possible to comprehensively "plan" the Soviet economy because neither was the information available nor could the instructions be fulfilled. It is not a question of imperfect planning, since a 100% correspondence of planning results with intentions is certainly unlikely, but rather that the actual fulfilment of the plans looks like a scatter diagram with a totally unexpected result making for shortages over the whole economy, and coexists with underemployed resources. I have, of course, argued this case in more detail in the pages of *Critique* (nos 1 and 2). Here I am only concerned to show that the administration which exists is a hybrid — to use Mandel's term — originally derived from planning, but distorted by market-like tendencies or by what I have called a law of self-interest, such that new forms of economic control have come into existence. Thus, for instance, the major allocation of resources has hitherto been arranged by a process of bargaining, which is hardly what "planning" is conceived to be. It bears some relation to different members of a cartel dividing up a market according to strength, but on the other hand the different ministries etc. are not in fact independent units yet.

The contradiction between planning and market laws

The original bureaucracy and now the Soviet élite have come to embody the contradiction which was at the heart of the NEP period. The problem is that whereas the competition between the state and private sector had to end with the victory of the one side or the other, i.e. with the victory of the law of value or law of planning, or with the success of either the proletariat or the bourgeoisie, the élite has contained the struggle within itself. In its bureaucratised form it has taken the verbal character within the USSR of a debate between those in favour of centralised planning with computerisation as against those in favour of a market controlled by the centre in a greater or lesser degree. Obviously there is a whole range of positions in this debate, but the extreme of "computer versus market" defines its limits. While it was a problem of extracting the maximum surplus to produce growth, however wasteful, exhortative planning or organisation proved a sufficient stimulus together with individual self-interest. But once the problem became one of the relative surplus, questions of productivity and technology moved to the fore. This was for two reasons.

The first reason was that the mixture of force and ideology could only operate for a limited historical time in the absence of direct material interest. The shift between town and country has provided the Soviet élite with an important historical hiatus, since the worker has been better off than his country cousin. The worker, however, had to be provided with some real return for his labour other than the absolute minimum. In its absence the only result would be the continued and progressive alienation of the worker from his workplace and not just from the system. The peasant, who has been permanently antagonised, may not have been important in direct political terms, but the low production of food was the primary problem and in fact remains such. Hence a means of improving the low productivity of agriculture was imperative in order to maintain and improve the productivity of the industrial worker. Finally the intelligentsia had to be requited not just because of their importance in production or the need to improve the efficiency of production, but above all because the régime had to establish a social base. This was not necessary while there was no hereditary proletariat on the scene. The régime had liquidated both the capitalist elements and the marxists. The rise of this proletariat immediately posed the need to broaden the social base of the élite. The special role of the intelligentsia and the economic reforms requires a separate discussion (see below).

The second reason was that the economy could not be run without more precise instruments, of a quality which would at least serve their original purpose. The constant shortages, unemployment of resources through hold-ups in production whether inside the plant or between plants, lack of spare parts, permanent concentration on department one goods to the detriment of department two, and other well-known phenomena, required solutions instead of exhortations. When there were few goods, the absence of spare parts was of less importance, just as a production hold-up could be more easily dealt with or ignored in an economy of relatively fewer and more primitive plants. The interconnections between the different sectors and enterprises have become progressively tighter. The growth of the economy therefore demanded more and more planning, but the centre has had no means to implement the objective requirements of the economy. The very size of Soviet plants, considerably greater than those in the USA, required closer co-ordination with the inputs and outputs of other Soviet plants. Trotsky once pointed out that the advantage of planning also meant the disadvantage that when a mistake was made the mistake then became, if it applied to the whole economy, of great importance. This has become more and more true. The worst aspect, perhaps, has been the continued failure of the Soviet system to incorporate new technology, new product mixes and new sectors or plants as an automatic mechanism built into the system.

Functions of the Soviet élite

Essentially I have argued that the sheer advantages of the organised form of production predominated over the colossal waste which occurred in the early period. Furthermore, the wasteful nature of this growth was masked by the continued high level of surplus pumped out of the working class. Politically the ending of this system coincided with Stalin's death, or rather the search for an alternative appeared to be more open after the dictator died. In the period since the ending of force and the decline of stalinist ideology the élite has moved from one expedient to another in order to deal with its economic problems. It has had to tack between the poles of its own internal contradiction — between the use of increased administrative methods and increasing control, whether through more centralisation or less centralisation, and the increased use of the law of value. Up to the present all methods have failed, whether in industry or agriculture. This has been graphically demonstrated with the international wheat deals and the inability to maintain the consumer goods targets for the current five-year plan. The administrative expedients are quite obviously doomed to failure as long as the interests of the individual unit and the private individual are to maximise his own return, whether monetary or otherwise, and so minimise his information flow up or down and reduce his individual responsibility for change to negative proportions, unless he can demonstrate some apparent success.

Even if there is no alternative in the form of direct administrative changes, the élite does perform some function. It forces alterations in structures and personnel, which must of necessity lead to changes in instructions and so "lubricate" the possibilities for change and flexibility which are so lacking in the administered system in the USSR. The problem is that it intensifies the already existing insecurity of the individual and so throws the burden of decision-making still more on the centre. It is in this sphere that it is necessary to understand the growth of interest and contacts with Western business schools. The administration of an enterprise is not a technical question but one intimately bound up with the class relations of the society. When, therefore, the USSR sets out to impart Western methods of running an enterprise, it is obtaining the most up-to-date ways of extracting the surplus from the worker. The fact that these methods are more modern does permit a degree of improvement within the system, but since the enterprise has no way of regenerating its administration it is thereafter permanently linked to the West in order to discover the current means of dealing with the new problems which arise. This has involved not just the export of exchange scholars or the import of Western business experts, but the need for the establishment of the whole enterprise by Western firms. Whatever the other reasons — and they are important — the construction of such plant is required precisely in order to establish the new method of running such a firm in the USSR. Thus the USSR has been importing market methods of management in order to phase out its previous historically derived system. The dependence which then develops on the West and first of all the USA is not simply technical. Given the importance of Western travel for members of the élite, this contact establishes a means of acquisition of scarce goods and thus the enrichment usual for this social group. Indeed, it provides a means of entry into the élite itself, so that the contact established by the individual reinforces the bond with the capitalist economy. It would be surprising if these individuals did not move to reproduce the circumstances of the managers with whom they come into contact in the West. In other words, they will provide an important reservoir of support for the introduction of the market.

Since it is objectively clear that market methods without a market are unlikely to succeed, the Soviet élite must be driven increasingly either to introduce the market or to obtain the elements lacking in the Soviet economy from the West. It is important, however, to realise that there is no mechanism whereby the importations from the West can be not merely copied but developed and overtaken. It is clear that market methods introduced into a non-market economy are likely either to stagnate or lead to a market. What is worse, however, is that the import of new technology and consumer goods is unlikely to lead, as in the case of Japan, to the USSR absorbing the techniques and developing them further. The reason for this has been well expressed as follows by Radovan Richta in Czechoslovakia:

"A hangover from these days [the period of industrialisation — H. T.] is the conviction that the scientific and technological revolution can be called into being by the self-same directive methods — by something in the nature of a technocratic procedure. But this stems from a misconception about the substance of the revolution, which is not just a structural shift that can be carried out by one simple operation, but involves a continuous, universal stream of structural changes, with a multidimensional dynamic as the very essence of its progress. . . . It is necessary that the dynamics of the productive forces be built into the social conditions of production, to the structure of interests in human life."[6]

I differ from the view expressed here in a number of respects, but its basic point is as true of the USSR as of Czechoslovakia. Whatever the Soviet imports, their effect will be a once-for-all result, and unless repeated will probably lead to stagnation, as these imports (whether of methods of administration or goods) fail to cope with changing requirements of the economy. Where I do not agree is that the reason for the economic change lies in terms of the scientific and technological revolution. This, of course, is the fashionable reason given by the Soviet authors of a five-volume work on management and planning;[7] the truth is, however, that the problems were always there but were masked for a time for the reasons given above. It was above all the social tensions in the society which demanded the change. To this we shall return below. In the second place the authors of this work clearly believe that the turn to the market will provide the necessary dynamic. This is then counterposed to the stress on organisation made by Gvishiani and Gatovskii.[8] The former points out how much the technological problems under capitalism are organisational, and the latter suggests organisational solutions such as the associations.

The technical reasons for the failure to introduce new technology are well known. Any target system risks being disrupted with the introduction of something new. This, of course, is as much the case under capitalism as in the USSR, but in the West the firm is either richly rewarded for the risk or suffers to the point of bankruptcy. Since the result is by nature unpredictable, the rewards have to be considerable. Furthermore, the very existence of failing firms permits the giant monopolies to choose the technologies most likely to succeed. Such a degree of rewards and penalties is impossible in either a planned system or one as inflexible as the USSR. Given the constraints on unemployment and the insecurity of the enterprise management, dependent for its income and position on its superiors, the rewards are more likely to become penalties. It is not much use to a firm manager to hear of extra bonuses being received by his successor. The self-interest of the management is then to reduce to a minimum any disruptions which might occur, and this means avoiding new technology as much as possible. For the worker, whose extra bonuses for such changes are minimal, it is quite obvious that he will have no interest in assisting the development of any new techniques. The important point is that without the possibility of dismissals and market control over costs, the actual expenses of the enterprise will increase. The ultimate reason, as I have argued, is the conflict of interest between the individual manager and worker as against the planner or organiser. This conflict is intractable, so that either the régime goes to the market or it turns to the West.

Results of co-operation with the West

It is thus not surprising that the USSR is turning to the West for whole plants to be constructed, as their own plants would not easily cope. It follows also that the existing demand must beget still bigger demand. This is not just a question of spare parts, though this is obviously important; the fact is that the inter-relation of enterprises requires that they be brought up to similar standards. The unevenness which is thus deepened in the Soviet economy must imperatively demand a solution through the increased import of technology.

This does not mean that the pattern imposed by the multi-national corporations on the less developed countries will become the norm for the USSR or Eastern Europe. The maintenance of the monopoly of foreign trade ensures that the power of the Soviet state confronts that of the German or US corporation. It is quite clear that such firms cannot impose a particular industrial structure by selecting what they are prepared to sell or controlling the information flow. In any event, it is not so much the transfer of written information as the direct import of skills and plant that is required. On the other hand, too, it is of considerable value to such firms to have a secure market during times of such uncertainty and decline in the West. Indeed, the bargaining power of the USSR has increased considerably in the last two years with the rise in price of raw materials.

Nonetheless, the nature of Soviet technological dependence is of a different nature. Sutton has documented the massive imports of Western technology from the time of the twenties.[9] Consistently with his cold war ideology, he argues that capitalism has essentially maintained support for the USSR by providing it with crucial technology which it could not have acquired otherwise. The advice for Washington is as clear as the views of Senator Jackson. The importance of this relationship, however, has varied, and it would be simplistic to argue that since the USSR has gone through differing attitudes to the import of technology it can change its view at the present according to party whim.

It has been argued that the same forces driving the state to economic reforms have also led to the move to the West. The economic reforms themselves, with the internal logic of moves to the market, either expressed directly by the reformers or by the state in terms of an evolution towards the increased use of the profit motive, have tended to stimulate the reproduction of market-type organisation. In other words a Soviet plant will import the production line as it stands in the West, without the controls provided by the trade unions. The move to greater efficiency naturally tends to look to more efficient economies associated with the market.

Nonetheless, the basic urgency for the import of foreign goods derives from the socio-economic scene. The economic reforms cannot proceed while they imply, as they must, higher prices to reduce demand, income differentiation to increase material incentives, and tighter control over the production line for both speed and quality. This will only worsen the workers' situation, and the élite have already observed both in the USSR itself and in Poland the consequences of rising prices. Although there have been various experiments and decrees on redeployment, they have in fact not proceeded very far with allowing what would amount to large-scale unemployment. The élite has, as a result, been forced on to the only path left — a turn to the West. This, however, represents only a surrogate solution. Still, it is a surrogate which can provide the necessary goods which might make the economic reforms more palatable. In other words, they could smooth the way to the market which is so desired by the reformers, both by obtaining the workers' passivity and by the direct links established with world capitalism. If it were simply a question of perfecting the system, however, urgency would not be on the order of the day.

The real problem in the USSR is that the intelligentsia are imperiously demanding a similar position to their Western brethren, while the working class is stirring. Durable consumer goods and food are the two necessities required which can be obtained from the West. It is not a question of a declining standard of living but rather of one rising too slowly for some and very little for others. It is the inequality in the society among social groups, towns and geographical regions, not to speak of the comparisons with the West, which causes the discontent. In the absence of democratic forms of expression and the difficulty of using force, increasing concessions have now to be made primarily to the intelligentsia, as the social force likely to support the élite against the working class. What the intelligentsia wants is the opportunity to exist as private individuals without the system of personal dependence. This a market form would successfully serve, but it must be a market with goods — and this is where the importance of trade with the West comes in.

The historical basis of the system has been exhausted; and because it can no longer get any return from administrative pressure but cannot turn to the market either, it has been compelled to resort to the compromise of market-like reforms combined with détente with the West. The big corporations of the West are well aware of the pressures on the Soviet leaders and hence are able to hold out for two strategies. The first amounts to the present situation that as the USSR becomes increasingly enmeshed in international trade and increasing amounts of US aid, it will willy-nilly be pushed along the road to the market. As I have argued, if sufficient amounts of aid are indeed available, this view will probably prove successful. This is for two reasons: that the import of Western capitalist techniques will only increase the appetite for still more, and secondly that the provision of sufficient consumer goods might make the economic reforms envisaged more palatable. The alternative strategy amounts to an attempt to bargain from the strength of knowing the USSR's weakness. To preserve its existence, the élite will be prepared to make political and economic concessions which strike at the heart of the social structure of the Soviet Union. The political concessions in terms of emigration we have already seen, but the US corporations are unlikely to make massive investments without significant concessions over control as well. This is not just a political act but a move of commercial prudence. It is well known that foreign firms have considerable problems in dealing with the local economic system, so leading to an escalation of costs and exten-

sion of time periods. At this moment the bargaining power of the
USSR has been enhanced by the rise in price of its exports, but
this is almost certaintly a temporary phenomenon.

What tends to maintain the pressure of the interconnection
between the Soviet economy and the West is the peculiar nature
of the trade with the West. The Soviet economy is geared to the
production of producer goods, but it exports raw materials in
large measure to the West. The present conjuncture has certainly
assisted it, but has not removed the pressure to export manufac-
tured goods to the West. As everyone knows, their goods are
invariably of lower quality and technical standard than those of
their international competitors. In order to deal with this situation, the régime in effect creates an export sector with a wider
range of incentives and stricter controls. They have, in fact, been
reasonably successful in selling their wares where it was possible
to sell them at low prices. Indeed, at some prices their goods do
become worth purchasing. The result, however, is to enhance
the export sector and increase the demands on the other, com-
plementary industries. Since the export sector is producing for a
market and its incentive system is more closely linked to economic
reform ideas, more and more sectors are thereby sucked into the
market or the economic reforms.[10]

This latter tendency is increased to the extent that trade and
aid missions permit comparisons between the availability of goods
and standards of living of managers East and West. The much
easier life and greater security of the Western manager is not lost
on his Eastern counterpart, who not unsurprisingly is drawn
towards market incentives, particularly for managers. One could
also argue that there should be less inequality and more democracy, but this is a socialist argument not popular in Eastern
Europe. The élitist position of the Soviet manager is the same
whether he is in a less developed country or in a more developed
one. The patent inefficiency of the USSR, with its lower standard
of living, was bound to cause those sections of the intelligentsia
which come into contact with the West to move to its support.

The overall result is that the Soviet demand for Western goods
is insatiable but the only way that they can be satisfied is through
Western credits.[11] This remains true whether the price of raw
materials goes up or down, though the bargaining position of the

USSR is greater in the former situation. There has, of course, been a vast increase in what amounts to Western aid[12] in the last few years, and we may expect it to increase. It is clear, however, that the days of wheat deals are probably over, though Soviet shortages are bound to recur. Should there be another such agricultural failure (and since they have occurred regularly, we should expect it), we must anticipate a greatly weakened USSR facing the USA. Then, with a considerable debt burden already on its shoulders, the USSR would have to give concessions of a more fundamental kind.

This last case is only one of many possibilities. The system may receive a shock from a number of sources. Another revolt or threatened revolt in Eastern Europe would again tax the régime to the point where it would make further concessions to the West. The source of the shock is not really important for the present argument, except in one case. This is where the economic reforms are pursued to their conclusion and the resulting discontent among the working class is not contained. In such an instance the régime may only survive through aid from the West, but it would then be a client state of the USA. This limiting example does illustrate the tendency in the world economy for the USSR to become increasingly dependent on the West, and particularly the USA as the dominant capitalist power. Dependence implies one-sidedness, and that is what it is, for the USSR élite requires precisely the consumer goods and technology to prop up its own social position, and only the USA or Germany can supply these. In other words the present economic reforms, partial as they are, represent a turn towards the one pole of the contradiction on which the élite is impaled; but since the other pole is necessarily implied, they are compelled to turn outside the society. Had the West been in the same relatively healthy economic state that it was in the sixties, it is very possible that the USSR might well have dissolved into a Yugoslav-type situation. Fortunately this is no longer the case, and the decline of capitalism in the next decade will very likely render it incapable of restoring the market in the USSR, while on the contrary the rise of working-class movements and possibly even states will pose a serious threat to the régime from quite another source.

NOTES

1. Michael Ellmann, *Economic Reform in the Soviet Union* (London 1969).
2. E. Preobrazhensky, *The New Economics* (London 1966), p. 127.
3. Ibid. p. 127.
4. Ibid. p. 259.
5. *Devyataya konferentsiya RKP (B)* : *Protokoly* (Moscow 1972), pp. 139-99.
6. R. Richta, "Dynamika doby a nase revoluce", *Rude Pravo*, 27 May 1966, quoted in J. Goldman and K. Kouba, *Economic Growth in Czechoslovakia* (New York 1969).
7. *Upravlenie, planirovanie i organizatsiya nauchnykh i tekhnicheskikh issledovanii* (Moscow 1970).
8. Ibid. Vol. 1, page 40 (Gvishiani) and pp. 102-22 (Gatovskii).
9. A. C. Sutton, *Western Technology and Soviet Economic Development* Vol. 1: 1917-30, Vol. 2: 1930-45 and Vol. 3: 1945-65, Stanford 1968, 1971 and 1973.
10. The interconnection between the reforms and foreign trade is explicitly recognised. Thus a recent article in *Vneshnaya torgovlaya* states that the import of Western technology serves not just to improve Soviet goods but also to permit higher quality exports and, secondly, assists the use of economic levers inside the USSR (V. Malkevich: *Vneshnaya torgovlaya* 9/74, p. 46).
11. The introduction of payment for Western projects inside the USSR with Soviet goods and the interconnection with foreign plants, as envisaged for instance in the treaty with France, will put increasing demands on the USSR to improve the quality and nature of its production outside this sector, as well as sucking in more imports. Either the treaty will break down or an imperative change will be demanded in line with the market economy.
12. The change of trade over the last few years illustrates this proposition; the deficit with the West has markedly increased, to around the one billion ruble mark. This is unprecedented, especially as it shows every sign of continuing. The Soviet-French treaty makes it clear, as other treaties do, that this trade will be financed through credit of up to ten years. (See *Vneshnaya torgovlaya SSSR*, 1973.)

4

Structural causes of the Soviet coexistence policy

ANTONIO CARLO

Leninism and peaceful coexistence

"The influence of the socialist world system upon struggles for liberation does not consist in promoting revolution but in something else.

Above all, socialism, thanks to the notable successes of socialist countries, exercises a growing influence upon the peoples of the world.

Capitalism cannot endure peaceful coexistence with socialism, because the socialist system offers incomparably greater possibilities for the development of productive forces and culture, for satisfying the material and intellectual needs of man and for promoting his developments in all areas. In the near future the USSR will have the highest living standard and the shortest working day in the world. That will, along with the policy of peace and friendship among peoples, tirelessly pursued by the USSR and the socalist states, contribute enormously to the growing attractive power of communist thought. This factor will exercise an increasingly greater influence not only upon the working class, but also upon the peasant masses, upon the intellectual class and upon the urban petty bourgeoisie, upon the victims of monopoly."[1]

Thus two Soviet ideologues define the policy of peaceful coexistence; this definition seems to me, in a "brutal" fashion, to be the clearest of all those which have been employed to describe this policy. The growth of a system of countries calling themselves "socialist" cannot be an impulse to revolution in countries still suppressed by capitalism; it merely opens a phase of "peaceful competition", at whose conclusion socialism will be victorious because it is economically stronger, just as (the comparison is mine) in the competitive capitalist market place the most able concerns are victorious. Doubtless national struggles of liberation also play a role in Soviet theory, but only a secondary one, subordinated to the primary and decisive element, the economic development of the USSR and other "socialist" countries. For more than fifteen years the Soviet Union has laboriously sought to maintain that this theory was in continuity with the thought of Lenin; in fact, Lenin was certainly aware (and the Chinese make the same point) that different social orders must coexist during a given period, but he did not ascribe the final victory of socialism either to the quantative development of productive forces in the USSR or to the greater capacity of Soviet planning. This means that Lenin did not borrow the competitive model of the capitalist market place to apply it to the world revolutionary process. His well-known comments on the Menshevik Sukhanov's book on the Russian revolution are indicative;[2] the Russian revolution broke out in a phase in which productive forces still required much in the way of development, but the proletariat, as Lenin polemically observes, cannot wait for this development — it seizes power in order to direct the economic process itself. Transferred to the present-day situation, it would follow that, for example, people of the third world do not have to wait some vague and ill-defined future in which the Soviet plan will have demonstrated its greater capacity: they can and must make their own revolution, if the social contradictions permit it, and one could say that these contradictions even break out where the development of productive forces has not reached a high level (as in Russia in 1917)[3] and where the revolutionary forces have not awaited the economic final victory of "socialist" countries (neither the Cubans, the Chinese nor the Vietnamese did this). This means that throughout the world the decisive factor in the development of socialist revolution is not the efficiency of Soviet planning but the struggle of the proletariat and of oppressed peoples, which feeds upon the socio-economic contradictions of imperialism. To reverse this point of view and place the requirements of the Soviet development of production in the foreground involves a complete sacrifice of the possibility of revolutionary struggle, and the true character of the non-leninist version of coexistence then clearly manifests itself: the class interests of the dominant Soviet ruling clique — which seeks its salvation by developing trade with the West in order to solve explosive internal problems — are to be ideologically disguised.

We have no great problem with formal orthodoxy; if it is true that practice is the criterion of truth, then the only orthodoxy we have to respect is that of reality. We would even be ready to accept the Soviet theses, if only they corresponded to reality (and thus to the interests of the masses). But if we look at things more closely, it is easy to see that there is no organic connection between the development of productive forces in the USSR and the development of socialist consciousness in the world. In the period from 1920 to 1940, when only a small minority of heretics (to whose opinions I subscribe) denied to the USSR the character of a socialist country, however distorted, and when the USSR was offered to the working masses as a socialist model, the Soviet plan recorded enormous successes, in comparison with a capitalism that was shaken to its foundations by the greatest depression in its history. And yet viewed politically, these were years of revolutionary defeat and unstoppable reaction, years when the Chinese revolution went on the defensive (a necessary but nonetheless defensive measure), years when (with the complicity of many) Spanish democracy was murdered, years in which nazism triumphed in Germany, embarking upon a huge policy of expansion.

After 1958-9, the situation changed fundamentally (irony of fate: just at the moment when theories of coexistence began to "bloom" in the USSR). The rich years for the Soviet Union were in the past. 1960 is the watershed, from which one can trace the slackening off of the average growth rate of Eastern European countries.[5] The Western countries experienced, with few exceptions, a boom which lasted for the entire 1960s. But in spite of some defeats, as in Indonesia, political developments proceeded quite differently: these were the years of Cuba (a socialist experiment 90 kilometres off the coast of the United States), the years of the French May and of the Italian Autumn, the years of the global spread of student protests and of the unprecedented radicalisation of Afro-Americans, the years when, following Cuba, a new socialist experiment was undertaken in the heart of the American imperialist hunting ground, Chile. The Cuban retreat and the temporary defeat of the Chilean people in no way diminish the great importance of these experiments. Just the fact that they were possible at all indicates the practical applicability of long unthinkable hypotheses, and consequently of new power relations on a world scale. We see that the development of Soviet production and the development of socialist revolution are in no way processes mechanically tied to one another, as economistic theorists of Soviet coexistence would have us believe.[6]

It is not, however, my intention to deny the importance of the Soviet world presence in relation to the aforementioned revolutionary processes. Even if, in my opinion, the USSR is no socialist country but rather one whose basis is a new form of human exploitation ("bureaucratic collectivism"),[7] the mere existence of a superpower whose interests do not immediately and generally agree with those of American imperialism obviously represents an obstacle to the absolute superiority of the USA, and the revolutionary forces of the world do well to utilise this contradiction for the sake of their own efforts. Nevertheless, the revolutionary successes which have occurred in recent years are in no way the results of a proven higher performance on the part of the Soviet economy, since these are exactly the years in which the structural weaknesses of the Soviet economic system have openly shown themselves.[8]

To this extent, the Soviet theory is "false", i.e. it corresponds to the interests of social groups different from the proletariat and antagonistic to it. Measured against reality, it reveals itself as a brake upon revolutionary movements which, even when they have known how to make use of the tactical conflict between the USSR and the USA,[9] have often collided with the interests of Soviet economic foreign policy. There is a really sensational example to illustrate the position of the USSR when the interests of popular liberation struggles conflict with the need to maintain good intergovernmental relations with the USA. The well-known expert on problems of the Cuban economy, Michel Gutelman, tells of an episode which happened around the middle of the 1960s. Cuba resolved to undertake a "dumping policy" with its sugar. A substantial part of Cuban sugar production is purchased by "socialist" countries, enabling Cuba to sell the remaining produce at low prices on the capitalist market. This "economic raiding" policy would have had devastating consequences for Latin American sugar producers and would have created economic tensions and social conflicts within the imperialist camp. But let Gutelman tell the story:

"Cuba thus decided to undertake a 'dumping policy' and to ignore the Latin American marginal producers. We can say that this policy was partially successful. It is, for example, a certain if not familiar fact that the unrest in Santo Domingo in 1965 emanated for the largest part from the unemployed, from agricultural workers from the sugar fields.

How did it occur? The owners of sugar refineries were compelled to shut them down because of low sugar prices in the world market that year, and the cane went uncut. Cuba's dumping policy, whose goal was to lower the price of sugar, thus had political consequences. The same is true of Argentina, in Tucuman province, where many problems depend upon unemployment arising from the fact that the sugar capitalists were compelled either to close down the refineries or at least limit the sugar harvest. It is clear that Cuba could openly pursue this policy.

How could it do it? Because Cuba sells seventy per cent of its sugar at 6 cents a pound to socialist countries, i.e. because only one part of its production is sold on the world market, in the capitalist market place. But neither the Dominican Republic nor Argentina, which sell their entire produce on the free market — or on a market preferred by them but still dependent upon the free market — could do the same. The Cuban dumping policy could therefore play a significant role. But can Cuba really implement this policy, which Fidel announced in a speech in 1965? Does Cuba have the necessary force to pursue such an aggressive and revolutionary policy on the world market? We reply no, Cuba by itself does not have the possibility for carrying through this policy. Cuba began a policy which exceeded her powers. Why? In Cuba, dollar investments are preferred in the sugar sector; therefore, there is an enormous need of dollars for

the development of sugar production. You cannot obtain
these dollars in the world market if you are pursuing a
dumping policy which leads to the lowering of prices. The
Cubans had no other choice than to turn to the Soviets and
say: 'in order to sell sugar to you, we must invest many
dollars in our economy, in our sugar sector; therefore, it
would be appropriate for you to pay for a part of the sugar
that we sell to you in dollars, since this sugar not only gives
us Soviet material, but also dollars, world currency.' This
means that the dumping policy of Cuba depends upon the
good will of the USSR, and in reality the latter is the key
to peaceful co-existence in the Latin American sugar market.

If the USSR is prepared to pay Cuba for a portion of its
sugar in dollars, Cuba can without further ado drive down
the price of sugar on the world market. But if the USSR is
unwilling, then Cuba will be compelled to find a means for
once again raising the price on the world market and
abandoning its dumping policy. What means does it have at
its disposal now? It consists in Cuba's subscribing to the
international sugar agreement, which has been discussed for
years. That means, to put it in plain words, that the USSR is
not willing to support Cuba's aggressive policy in the world
market."[10]

As one can see, its concern about good political and economic
relations with the West led the USSR to throttle a highly effective
form of economic struggle. The Cubans by no means expected a
gift from the Russians, but only another condition of payment for
a portion of their sugar production — a form of assistance which
certainly would not have been impossible for the USSR. The
expansion of trade with the West (unattainable in a politically
tense situation) is, as we shall see, of decisive significance for the
USSR, since it seeks to solve or diminish dysfunctions of planning
in this way. The demands of the Soviet economy repress those
of revolutionary action, of an action which would also be possible
from the viewpoint of trade relations, since dumping is a generally
recognised form of competition in the capitalist world market.[11]

Certainly one could discuss specific points of the Cuban tactic:
for example, it is conceivable that unemployed workers in the

sugar fields would be influenced by anti-socialist propaganda, if one did not work with them politically and explain to them that their dismissal resulted less from dumping than from the logic of profit, the crisis of which had provoked the Cuban policy. Nevertheless, the fact that the unrest in the Dominican Republic in 1965 bore an anti-imperialist character is evidence that one could combat whatever propaganda the enemy had to offer. To change or call in question a tactic which has been proven in practice, in order to give it a more effective form, is something quite different from brutally strangling it. This illustration reveals Cuba's gradual turning away from internationalist commitment at the same time as an alarming internal involution.[12]

Naturally, Soviet pressure has not always been crowned with rapid success. Relations to revolutionary movements are dialectical and not mechanical. Relations differ from one situation to another, and consequently one's negotiating strength with the USSR differs as well, often compelling the USSR to take up less openly reactionary positions. (It was impossible to abandon Vietnam because of political pressure on the part of the Chinese, although the real history of Soviet pressure on Hanoi remains to be written.) The third disturbing factor for peaceful coexistence are the people of the world, and both of the superpowers must deal with them at the permanent negotiations that they have carried on since Camp David. In spite of the conflicts which are constantly reappearing, these permanent negotiations are an index to events of the last fifteen years.

Continuity and change in Soviet foreign policy

There is a great temptation on the new left and among the old anti-stalinist opposition (trotskyists), in the face of the permanent negotiations between the two superpowers, to seek the causes of present coexistence in the theory of socialism in one country. One thus produces a binding continuity in foreign policy between the Stalin era and the following period. Livio Maitan, a leading member of the Fourth International, writes:

"From 1934 on, the popular front corresponded exactly to Soviet foreign policy; after Stalin had settled accounts with the kulaks, he proceeded to strengthen the bureaucracy by

means of massive purges, whose high point was reached in a
a systematic liquidation of the leninist old guard. Reconsolidation within was tied to reconsolidation on an inter-
tional level, i.e. to the introduction of relations whose aim
was, to employ the current expression, "détente" with some
of the biggest capitalist powers."[13]

My own opinion is that in spite of the continuity in economic
structure which ties Stalin's Russia to that of the following
period, there exist fundamental differences in foreign policy: the
economic structures, despite their unchanging regularities, point
to different developmental phases which could very well require
different lines in foreign policy. In particular there seems to me,
even phenomenologically, to be a difference between the 1928-
1953 period and the 1959-1974 period, in which the years
between 1953 and 1959 are a period of gradual transition. The
foreign policy of the USSR in its stalinist phase is characterised
by a high degree of flexibility. One goes from the extremist position (the "social fascism" theory) of the years 1928-1934 to the
moderate one of 1934-39, ending with a brusque turn in the
Stalin-Hitler pact. After the alliance with the West imposed by
Hitler's attack, in the post-war period the USSR by and large
presented a defensive (see the attitude to the Chinese revolution)
but nonetheless "hard" line, which is very different from that of
the present day policy of coexistence. This policy of coexistence
has brought the Soviets to the point that they did not even wince
when American bombs almost fell on Kosygin's head during his
visit to Hanoi. We need only contrast this with the events in
Prague in 1948 and especially the Berlin blockade, which was a
resolute answer to the aggressive policies of the West in a period
when the latter possessed the monopoly on atomic weapons (the
first Soviet nuclear weapon was set off in September 1949), and
when the USSR had to bear the heavy load of reconstruction.
No similar positions have been adopted since the Khrushchev era.
Even the Cuban missile crisis cannot be compared with the Berlin
blockade. Caught in the act, the Soviets hastily changed their
position without even the least attempt at a confrontation, in
spite of the absurdity of the American demand: Cuba is a
sovereign state, and the USSR had not threatened to attack the

United States because of its military installations in Turkey. Even in the U-2 crisis, Khrushchev's sensational and theatrical reactions did not call the "dialogue" in question, at least not seriously.

In spite of the contradictory policy of the Stalin era, the different phases of foreign policy up to 1953 are connected with each other by an element of continuity: the need to defend the Soviet state and its underlying economic order. One might find such an observation banal, since every foreign policy is determined by this factor. But my proposition is that the exclusive and decisive interest which guided foreign policy during the Stalin era was that of defending the Soviet state at an international level; from an *economic* point of view, the Soviet system maintained and developed itself, doubtless with some contradictions, but without needing comprehensive trade relations with the West. The Russians certainly profited from the great depression and made a couple of good deals, but foreign trade played an almost insignificant role in their economic policy.[14] With the Khrushchev era the situation changed: the latent contradictions which had not broken out in the preceding phase now clearly emerged, and presented the Soviet leadership with the problem of establishing better relations with the West in order to eliminate the more dangerous structural dysfunctions by means of foreign trade.

The chief motive behind Soviet relations with other states during the Stalin era had been an immediately political one; economics determines politics in the last instance, and the interest in guaranteeing the political and military security of the USSR was, in spite of everything, determined by the need to secure the socio-economic structure and its dominant class (the central political bureaucracy), although this was indirectly mediated. In this phase there was a multiple and tactically flexible policy, by which national defence was secured in different ways, with the help of various combinations and alliances. In the 1928-32 period, when acute tensions dominated the USSR and an imperialist attack was feared, the extremism of the foreign policy of the USSR and the Comintern was necessary as a weapon to threaten capitalist countries: if you attack us, we will react by stirring up revolution.[15] In the 1934-39 period, one can explain the turn from the popular front to the policy of coexistence for the reasons

adduced by Maitan. And the flirtation with Hitler had its origins
in the cold attitude of the West (especially France and England)
towards Stalin, and in the simultaneous weakness of the USSR in
relation to Hitler. This motivated Stalin, especially when faced
with the French-English attitude, to seek the treaty with his arch-
enemy.

In the Khrushchev era the interests of the economic structure
directly asserted themselves in foreign policy, and limited the
negotiating room of Soviet delegations. The demands of the
economy, which once again raised the question of expanding trade
with the West, formed a constant. The margin of tactical elasticity which had previously existed was drastically curtailed, since
the West was far more united than it had been in the past by a
domineering superpower, the USA. This explains the relative
stability of Soviet foreign policy after Camp David, a stability
which fundamentally differs from the extraordinary ups and downs
of the Stalin era.

Foundations and development of the Soviet economy

The causes for the deterioration of Soviet society lie in the past,
in the final years of the leninist period. In fact, in 1919-20 a
dramatic situation came about: the civil war and the ensuing
economic crisis (the volume of production had sunk to 13% of
its 1913 level) resulted in the substantial disappearance of the
proletariat, whose best cadres had been absorbed by the Red
Army or the bureaucracy and were thus divided from their class.
Deprived of their basis, the soviets were sapped dry, and political
power concentrated itself in an exclusive party élite which fused
with the state; this élite rose from the ruins of a disintegrating
bourgeois society in which there was no longer a proletarian force
that could rule the state.

The "bonapartisation" of the Soviet state, about which so much
has been written, took place during 1928-29, just as a jump in
development occurred. The difficult situation in the USSR,
threatened from without by imperialist aggression and from within
by the economic sabotage of the kulaks and NEP officials, raised
the question: how could a mechanism of industrial development
be put into operation which would enable the USSR to fight

external aggression and liquidate the enemy within? The only force capable of realising this programme was the political élite, the state and party bureaucracies, which continued their fusion and in 1928-29, with global planning and the collectivisation of agricultural, gained authority over the economic apparatus and so became a class (in a marxist sense) which thus centralised political power and property in their hands.

The system which subsequently developed I have called bureaucratic collectivism — borrowing the terminology (while limiting its content) from Bruno Rizzi.[16] This formation is a socio-historic one, based upon exploitation, but different from capitalism, from which it is distinguished by its static as well as its dynamic traits: (1) one class, which we must consider as a collectivity — and not individual members or groups as in capitalism — possesses the basic means of production; (2) the development of the economy is carried on by central planning and not, as in capitalism, by free competition among different production units, each concerned with maximising its own profits ;(3) enlarged reproduction affects use value (and not exchange value, as in capitalism) and produces a constant, extraordinary and incurable favouring of the primary (capital goods) sector; (4) the relations of distribution, by means of which exploitation is realised, are essentially independent of the market and centrally determined; (5) there is an organic concentration of political power and property — a concentration lacking in capitalism, which maintains a difference of roles (between "citizen" and "bourgeois", in Marx's words) that only occasionally coincide in one and the same person.

The foregoing are the structural characteristics of the system that went through a crisis after Stalin's death. The causes of this crisis were as follows. In the "heroic" period of stalinist expansion it was (relatively) easy to plan; the aim of the system was to develop sector I of industry (investment goods),[17] in order to guarantee the economic self-sufficiency and politico-military independence of the USSR and the new ruling class. Once sector I had been developed, sector II (consumer goods) and the agricultural economy had also to be developed. Once the USSR had become a power which participated in 20% of world industrial production, it could no longer produce enormous quantities of steel for the sake of producing machines whose function was to produce more steel. An economy which favoured sector I to such an extent inevitably involved social and political tensions which remained latent under Stalin and rose to the surface after his death with the so-called "consumer strikes". In these strikes, Soviet workers refused to buy the junk produced by the under-developed sector II. The task of adequately organising production and overcoming the unbalanced structure of the Stalin era proved to be impossible in the USSR.

To understand the causes of this weakness, one must know that even in Stalin's time everything was not centrally overseen: certain micro-economic decisions could only adequately be reached by the plant directorship, the managers, who were themselves tied to the general directives of the plan (which were often quite detailed). Failure to fulfil his production quota would have had catastrophic consequences for the manager, so he often utilised plant autonomy in order to fulfil the plan by means of "short-cuts" which were frequently on the edge of illegality. If the quota was determined by weight, one produced extremely heavy trucks, tractors, lampshades, nails, paper etc., which were thus of inferior quality and not very functional. If the planner reacted to this trick and determined the quota for paper according to square metres and that for nails according to finished articles, from now on the nails would be as small as possible and the paper extremely thin and brittle. With the quantitative but imbalanced expansion of production, the problem of planning grew too. The multiplication of production units led to an extraordinary increase of difficulties in calculation. In the 1960s it was estimated that if planning was continued in the same fashion, a million computers with a speed of 30,000 operations per second would have to calculate for several years uninterruptedly in order to elaborate a gigantic mathematical model with a million equations.

This was inconceivable, for economic, political and scientific reasons. But on the other hand, to make a decision to find out the needs of the economy by real participation of the masses (socialist democracy) would have been suicidal from a class standpoint. There was nothing to do but to expand the autonomy of the factory directorate by introducing the principles of market economy. We thus arrive, after a series of experiments following Stalin's death, at the ratification of the Kosygin Reform of 1965, whose main characteristic was a certain decentralisation of the market, with the reins of the economy left in the hands of the bureaucrats.

But conceding greater authority to the managers carries great risks for the bureaucracy. Because of his historical experience, the technocrat had been educated to give first place to the fulfilment of his production quota, since his success depended upon it — and this also led him, for the sake of fulfilling the plan, to employ the measures described above which were, however, damaging for the economy as a whole. The ideal of this group, socially privileged but subordinate to the bureaucracy and equipped by its specific historical formation with a particular outlook, is an economy which functions on the basis of decisions reached by the production units, and thus by the managers themselves — in other words, a capitalist economy. This latter functions on the basis of competition among various autonomous production units, the plan and the function of the state being subordinated to the market and to the production units operating within it.[18] In fact, the restoration of capitalism in the ruins of bureaucratic collectivism is an unavowed but real ideal of the managers. The polemics about the commercialisation of the Soviet economy which have raged for more than twelve years obscure a confrontation between bureaucrats and technocrats in which what is at stake is the transfer of power to the technocrats, the expropriation of the bureaucrats, and the restoration of capitalism.

The 1965 reforms were a partial and limited victory for the technocrats. In practice, however, it is clear that the principles of the market economy function badly under the domination of bureaucratic planning. In reality, the five-year plan for 1966-70 was a failure. The bureaucracy itself went over to the counter-attack and rescinded a large part of the reforms. In the Eastern bloc countries, where the reforms had already gone too far, historic and now notorious events took place.

We must analyse Soviet foreign policy in relation to the growing socio-economic tensions inside the USSR. The economy no longer develops according to the quantitative dimensions of the past. The system would require technological modernisation in order to produce consumer goods, and a minimum of popular assent for it to regain power. The low productivity of human labour power and the generally low level of productivity is an additional evil of the system.[19] Russian industry, plagued by problems of the inferior quality of manufacturing goods, cannot produce modern equipment on an adequate scale. For planning — even the increasingly inadequate Soviet type — one needs a certain number of computers, but the USSR still lags behind the West in this respect. If a given economic sector does not fulfil its production goals, which happens with increasing frequency, it can be necessary or useful to turn to the world market as a means of hindering the growth of tensions and dissatisfaction inside the country.[20] The import of agricultural produce from the West at the beginning of the 1960s is a well-known example.

The growth of these problems made peaceful coexistence, which determines the development of economic relations with the West, an essential and permanent component of Soviet policy after Stalin.

Peaceful coexistence, economic necessity and foreign trade with the West

"In the last half decade, the USSR's trade with capitalist countries, beginning with Finland, France, Italy, Japan, England and Sweden, has grown by more than half. The trade relations of the West with the USSR are not free from artificial restrictions. In many countries duties on Soviet goods are still very high. The USA attempts to undermine the development of the USSR's trade relations with other countries — but these attempts have been unsuccessful. Such an attitude can only strengthen the USA's other than enviable reputation as being a country which, in the twentieth century, aims at blocking the development of the international market.

Confronted with the objective necessity of the international division of labour, the structure of Soviet exports will increasingly correspond to the actual structure of our economy and to its possibilities.

If our trade partners will take account of the changes which have occurred and will continue to occur in the Soviet national economy, it will be possible for us to increase the amount of our imports from capitalist countries. We are of the opinion that long-range trade and credit agreements, showing an interest in stable, reciprocally advantageous trade relations with the USSR, will contribute more than in the past to developing imports.

It becomes ever clearer that the technical and scientific revolution which we face today requires freer international trade relations and lays the foundations for a broad exchange between the socialist countries and the countries of the capitalist system. This process can, in its own right, have a positive effect upon the international situation.

During the last half-decade, foreign trade has offered us the possibility of complying with important economic problems. But we are still far from having completely exhausted economic relations with the West. It is time that we re-evaluated the role of foreign trade. Often the functionaries of the foreign trade office retreat within their own sphere and are not sufficiently aware that their activities must be subordinated to intensifying the capacity of the national economy as a whole. Understandably, the long-range plan in the area of foreign trade cannot take account of all possibilities and of changes which occur in the world market. But just for that reason it is extremely important for foreign trade functionaries to have precise knowledge of the demands of our economy, to give free play to their spirit of initiative in making the most advantageous sales and purchases. On the other hand, representatives of industry often look at foreign trade as something of secondary importance. This absolutely false point of view must be changed and contact between industry and foreign trade increased.

In the new five-year plan we must foresee measures for improving the variety of exports and imports, for increasing their efficiency, for improving the quality of export goods, for perfecting methods of trade and for better utilising imported goods. We expect a significant increase in the extent of our exports and their effect. Therefore, it is necessary to give first place to developing the export of machinery, as well as developing the export of raw materials, partially finished products and other goods, which guarantee a high inflow of foreign currency."[21]

Out of this excerpt from Kosygin's report to the twenty-third congress of the Communist Party of the Soviet Union in 1966, the following elements emerge: (a) the growing importance of trade with the West; (b) the need to improve this trade by overcoming the hostile attitude of the USA and thereby securing coexistence; (c) the low efficiency of planning and of the Soviet directors, who are guided by the opinion produced in the preceding phase that foreign trade is unimportant, a notion which is completely out of date; (d) priority to developing exports of machinery.

Five years later, Kosygin's new report confirmed the development and growing importance of foreign trade in general and with the West in particular; he did not exclude an improvement in relations with the USA.[22] The official declarations of the Soviet leadership were reinforced by statistics.[23] In 1950, 83% of Soviet exports went to "socialist" countries, which accounted for 78% of Soviet imports; in 1970, both imports and exports accounted for 65%, the remainder being divided among wealthy capitalist countries and the third world.[24] Today, neo-capitalist countries account for 24% of all Soviet imports and 19% of its exports.[25]

Apart from these figures, the particular data relating to machines and equipment essential for the modernisation of Soviet factories are interesting. In 1970, the exports of this sector accounted for 22% of exports as a whole (2,482 million rubles against 1,029 million rubles in 1960), while imports accounted for 35% of Russian imports as a whole in this year, amounting to 10,565 million rubles. This sector has been running up a deficit, something which seriously bothers the Soviet leadership, because stagnation is making itself felt in this sector.[26] In 1960, the export of equipment amounted to 20.7% of exports as a whole, against 31% of total imports; in 1965, it was 20% against 34%; in 1971, 21.8% against 34%. As one can see, the USSR's ability to compete with foreign nations is very low.

Even more informative is the allocation of Russian machine exports in the year 1970, which is quite typical; of 2,482 million rubles, 72% went to Comecon countries (tied to the USSR by preferential agreements), 25% to underdeveloped capitalist countries whose backwardness created a demand for the products of Soviet technology, and finally 3% to capitalist countries, which have practically no interest in Soviet machinery.[27]

The structure of foreign trade emphasises the qualitatively low competitive ability of Soviet production in relation to the neo-capitalist West; this is underlined by the fact that the balance of trade with highly developed countries in recent years has very often run into a deficit.[28] A not insignificant portion of imports of equipment comes from monopolistic capitalist countries.

Of special interest is the relation to two countries which represent the highest and lowest step in the scale of neo-capitalist countries: United States and Italy. The official newspaper of the Italian Communist Party commented as follows on the agreement concluded during Nixon's trip to Moscow in June 1974:

> "In the realm of the possible, it was emphasised that the export of plant and technology from the USA to the USSR should continue to develop. As agreed, the Soviets want to pay with products produced in factories financed with American credits. Treaties which set forth guidelines for the delivery of American machinery for the truck factory which the USSR is building on the Kama will play a particular role in the development of economic relations.
>
> The factory, which will be one of the largest in the world and will produce heavy duty trucks for transport in the undeveloped regions of Siberia, will absorb a large part of the credits (200 million dollars in 1973) and by the end of the year climb to 300-400 million dollars. . . . For their part, official sources emphasised, the Soviets will supply the United States with numerous raw materials: precious metals, platinum, gems, non-ferrous metals as well as petroleum."[29]

The USSR acquires technology, paid for in the first place with raw materials and in the second with commodities, which are produced in factories built with decisive contributions from the Americans. One perceives the kind of relation that prevails between a neo-capitalist and a backward country. It now becomes clear why the USSR is often referred to as the underdeveloped superpower. In the case of Italy, things look somewhat different: in 1970, the surplus in the Italian balance of trade was 16.5 billion lire, and the total volume of mutual exchange accounted for 368.3 billion lire, as against 76.7 billion in the year 1959 when the policy of détente, planned for in the preceding five-year plan, began. Italy imports products from the Soviet iron and steel industry, Soviety machinery and, to a lesser extent, means of transport (less than 10% of the Italian import), while Italy's exports in this sector make up not less than 124 billion lire out of total exports of 192.4 billion lire.

But in the case of the chemical and textile sectors, comparison with the USSR can only be called shameful. The Soviets export chemical products to the value of 1,653 million lire and textile products to the value of 8,010 million lire, while they import chemical products to the value of 18 billion and textile products to the value of 31 billion lire. The USSR maintains its balance of trade with petroleum and its derivatives, minerals and scrap, which together account for roughly 125 billion lire in a total volume of 175.9 billion lire-worth of Soviet exports to Italy.[30]

The thirst for plans and highly developed technology explains the agreement with Fiat for Togliattigrad, with the Japanese for the exploitation of Siberia, or the attempted agreement with IBM for computers (the agreement would have been similar to that with Fiat) — an attempt which had to be abandoned in 1970 because of massive pressure by the American government upon IBM.

We find exactly the same situation, if in different dimensions, in the other countries of Eastern Europe. The German Democratic Republic, the most economically fertile country in Eastern Europe (we hear increasing talk of an East German *Wirtschaftswunder*), also shows an unequivocal qualitative production lag in comparison to the West. Its relations with the Federal Republic of Germany, its most important capitalist trading partner, are informative. West Germany occupies the second place in imports to, and fourth place in exports from, East Germany. The leading branch of East German industry is metal working, which accounts for 56% of its exports (1970), but only 11% of its exports to West Germany, while by contrast the West German export of metallurgical industry commodities makes up 49% of its total exports to East Germany, showing how little competitive ability East German industry has in its leading branch.[31]

The bottlenecks in Soviet foreign trade

Soviet trade with the West, characterised by the structure

described above, developed as a consequence of the policy of peaceful coexistence. But the volume of trade is still far from being adequate to the demands of the Soviet economy and to the expectations of the planners. In recent times, the latter have repeatedly complained about the backwardness and low efficiency of Soviet trade, which is not at a peak of development.[32] The degree of readiness on the part of the USSR to expand its trade relations with the West in the sector of the investment goods industry and of technology reveals itself indirectly through its relations with Czechoslovakia, an East European country that would offer better products if it did not have to compete with the West: [33]

"In the half-decade 1966-70, Czechoslovakia has imported nearly all of its required supply of petroleum and petroleum products from the USSR, as well as 90% of its grain, 87% of its aluminium, 82% of its iron-ore, 72% of its copper and 54% of its cotton, and has supplied the USSR with 20% of its requirements in machine and industrial plants as well as a large part of the equipment required for the extraction and long-range transport of solid and liquid minerals.

The trade agreement in effect between the two countries during the five-year period 1971-1975 foresees a total exchange to the extent of 13.5 million rubles — 143% of the volume realised in the preceding five years. The USSR will supply Czechoslovakia with 12 million tons of coal, 30,000 tons of aluminium, 163,000 tons of copper, 300,000 tons of cotton, 4,200 tractors, 3,000 machine tools, its entire supply of butter and corn, and 40% of its total supply of meat; Czechoslovakia will supply the USSR with 4,500 machine tools, 446 electric locomotive engines, 888 diesel ranger locomotives, 4,650 streetcar and trolley carriages, 300,000 motor-cycles and teams of technicians and trained personnel for carrying out industrial projects in the USSR."[34]

As we can see, Czechoslovakia is one of the most important trading partners of the USSR, something which casts a new light upon the Soviet intervention in 1968.[35] This small country exports technology and imports raw materials and agricultural products, but we can see the Soviet weakness: Czechoslovakia is also a country of "bureaucratic collectivism", which shows dysfunctions similar to those of the USSR. In another article[36] I have shown how at the beginning of the 1960s the Czech situation was characterised by a severe economic crisis (waste, low labour productivity, inferior quality of products, etc.), and it was just this crisis and the need to deal with it which led to the use of techno-cratic and marketing tendencies with all their well-known consequences. The Soviet invasion did not solve the problems of this economy; there are certain contradictions which cannot be resolved by resorting to tanks. One can thus understand better the Soviet hunger for technological products, which are acquired anywhere — the main consideration being that they are better than what is produced at home.[37] Naturally, the USSR would be happy if it could exchange imports from Czechoslovakia against imports from the advanced West; but in order to do so, it must get around certain bottlenecks in its own economy.

The first bottleneck consists, as we have seen, in the inefficiency of sectoral planning, frequently mentioned in the USSR. This inefficiency is not only a relic of stalinism, but an expression of the growing difficulties in co-ordinating the different branches of the economy in relation to the existing level of development, difficulties which one can especially observe in sectors in which the international market requires far greater elasticity than is possible for unwieldly and rigid Soviet planning. Because of these negative characteristics, absurd situations frequently arise.[38]

The most important bottleneck, however, remains the qualita-tively and quantitatively low productivity of labour in the Soviet economy, which is decisive in the West's lack of interest in an expansion of East-West trade. Even the Soviet leaders themselves, beginning with Kosygin, do not deny the significance of the problem.[39] Let us once again listen to a high Soviet official respon-sible for exports:

> "My own personal observations confirm what I have previously said. Within a period of less than six months, the Japanese have constructed a factory for the production of silicon on the basis of a Soviet licence. Some of our organisa-tions would require two years or more for the same factory. . . .[40] We have carefully examined the surface of the

castings, the shafts and other places in order to test their quality. We knew, and particularly myself as a smelter, where to look for defects in the alloys. But we could not find a single one. The plant director, attentive to our efforts, told us that we would waste time and unnecessarily strain our eyes, since we would never find any defective alloys there."[41]

After a brief interchange between the Soviet and the Japanese, the report continues:

"After this exchange of words, I armed myself with a magnifying glass and began to examine the welded seams with greatest attention, trying out the inside of the pieces with my hand, down into the corners. The result was always the same: the welds were perfect, there was no trace of burning or sand to be seen, even the surface did not have a single scratch. One could only congratulate the workers and engineers who had done such a good job. At the same time we were dumbfounded to think that in many of our factories the alloy division could not produce a single piece of such high quality. The same is even true of the "Stankolit" in Moscow, and I hope the comrades in the factory will not take offence at this. One might think that this high quality had been guaranteed by an astonishing technical performance on the part of the division, by mechanisation and, where possible, by automisation. Later we saw that it was a completely normal workshop, equipped with normal machinery, such as one would find in the majority of our own workshops."[42]

The stupefaction of the Soviet Vice-Minister for Foreign Trade — since he was the person in question — and his obvious humiliation show better than any statistics, which say nothing about quality, the enormous backwardness of the USSR in this area, all the more so since we have here an example from the primary sector, which is always the most favoured in the USSR. But as we have seen, such kinds of dysfunction are structural, since they are a result of the centrifugal tendency of the plants (of the managers) in relation to the plan, a tendency which will increase with the growing incapability of central economic planning.

The commercialisation of the economy offers no solution, since a wholesale adoption of market principles within bureaucratic collectivism would disturb its equilibrium and possibly lead to a restoration of capitalism. Blocking reforms or delaying their execution, as has been done, is also no solution, since one cannot solve a problem by resorting to whatever has caused the problem in the first place.

The USSR has no other choice than to look for indirect solutions, of which the one so far employed consists in exchanging raw materials (there is no quality problem here) against technology.[43] But this is an expedient which the USSR finds less than satisfying: it constantly reverts to the absolute priority of machine exports, a field in which it decisively lags behind.[44]

The reason for the dissatisfaction with this solution is clear: the USSR itself is a major consumer of raw materials, being a country which represents 20% of world industrial production. In particular, the USSR needs its enormous energy and mineral resources for its own use, the more so since the imperialist multi-national concerns control the unlimited reserves of the third world, almost completely excluding the USSR. And we must bear in mind the fact that Russian products, apart from their inferior quality, include a high percentage of junk or short-lived products. The Soviet industry which produces lampshades, tractors or nails does not consume, it over-consumes, and it wastes raw materials; this is an additional limitation to the export of raw materials to the West.

One indirect solution could therefore be to increase the prices of raw materials, which would enable the USSR to import more without simultaneously extending the export of raw materials. But the creation of a consortium of oil-producing countries, as the well-known expert on the third world, Pierre Jalée, has observed, cannot be repeated in the case of other raw materials. In addition, it is doubtful whether the USSR could successfully stoke up the fires of rebellion in the third world. The weak national bourgeoisies in these countries are too corrupt to be able to stand up to the imperialism to which they are tied. It is no accident that the Iranians have let it be known that they will invest the larger part of their surplus from petroleum in the West. The bourgeoisie would have to mobilise the masses with a courageous policy of reform — but that would be cutting its own throat. Moreover, one must take into consideration the fact that Soviet help and co-operation could in no way replace the by no means disinterested but vital assistance from the West.

Chile's socialist president, Allende, once said:

> "Chile cannot supply its own needs, it much purchase machines, engines, petroleum, replacement parts and raw materials. Some people will say: 'Then buy them in the socialist world'. That is not possible, because it does not produce them."

We must understand the statement of the heroic socialist president in a limited sense: the socialist world does produce raw materials and machines, except that they are of inferior quality and limited variety, for which economic co-operation cannot always compensate. The third world countries and their ruling régimes are aware of this. Because of their backwardness they accept inefficient Soviet products, but their preferred trade partner remains the West, whose co-operation requires a high price but is more efficient; the rapid change of positions of certain régimes in the Middle East after Kissinger's and Nixon's shuttle diplomacy were very suggestive. Nevertheless, the Soviets are not at all squeamish, and when it comes to political pressure they are anything but weak, as the Cuban example cited above shows. Relations with the USA would deteriorate if the USSR were too openly to support certain struggles for independence in the third world; the Soviets know this, and once prevented the Cubans from exporting revolution.

In conclusion, we can say that the situation of the USSR is highly contradictory. They must have trade with the West, but it cannot grow in proportion to their needs; one can understand the extreme care with which the Soviet leaders gamble with what they have already won. This caution went so far as to take Kissinger's successes in the Middle East into the bargain, without batting an eyelid, as long as they were able to conclude a good trade agreement with the USA. This caution also led it to throttle Cuba's foreign policy, to remain cool when American bombs almost fell upon Kosygin's head during his visit in Hanoi, to accept a historic split within the international communist movement, etc.[48]

Contradictions in the Soviet economy, foreign trade and the policy
of coexistence

The Soviet policy of détente cannot possibly solve the problems of
the Russian economy; but from the point of view of the interests
of the dominant class in the USSR there is no alternative. The
foreign trade of any country is dialectically tied to its internal
economic problems, and reacts to these with greater or lesser
intensity, according to circumstances. Seen in this light, the situation has seemingly changed in comparison with the Stalin period,
a fact which equally concerns the effects of trade with the neo-
capitalist West upon the Soviet economic structure.

If the USSR were predominantly to import raw materials from
the West, it would have no major problems. "Capitalist" petroleum is no different from "socialist" petroleum. Even the import
of certain types of machines or parts would offer no great difficulties: a "capitalist" lathe that sits in a factory alongside ten
"socialist" lathes would have no great effect upon the social
structure.

But the situation changes when one begins to import entire
plants. A factory is not the sum of different machines, separated
from each other, but a qualitatively different state of affairs: what
is most important in a factory is its organisation, which is not
neutral but follows a given economic logic of direction. There is
no such thing as an economic ability to perform "in and of itself":
the factory exists only in relation to a given socio-historical
system. If the USSR buys plants, or lets Italian or American technicians construct them, these are capitalist factories and in no
way neutral. The productivity of these factories depends upon
specific social factors such as the organisation of labour, work
rates, wage structure and consumption. In the eyes of their
colleagues from the East, workers from the West work at an
unbelievable pace, and this is easily explained: the worker who
rebels against the laws of capitalist organisation is discharged
without further ado. Outside the gates stands someone who is
unemployed or a migrant labourer from one of the underdeveloped
countries, ready to replace him. Along with this ferocious competition and exploitation there is a level of consumption and
wages that is high in comparison with East European countries

and corresponds to the interests of capital; in highly developed Western countries, the sore point of the economy is sector II.

In the USSR the situation looks completely different. Economic development in the USSR was extensive and not intensive. The comparatively backward technology (in relation to the West) forced development to depend upon a high expenditure of labour power. In 1970, 48% of the population of the USSR worked. And if timid, limited reforms have provoked outbreaks of unemployment, they are nevertheless still quite insignificant.[49] Real Soviet unemployment is of a so-called fictional kind, characterised by the fact that workers, sure of finding a new job because of the high demand for labour power, give up their old job and wait for a new one; in certain periods this kind of unemployment has included up to 2.6% of the labour force.[50]

The pressure of potentially long-lasting unemployment does not affect the Soviet worker; in this regard, he is far better off than his colleague in the West. On the other hand, because the system cannot adequately stimulate sector II, it cannot satisfactorily develop either consumer goods or wages. The single instrument for integrating the working class consists in slowing down the pace of work and in relatively short working hours. As things presently stand, it is clear that Soviet factories operating in the USSR are not a going concern in the long run. Capitalist factories achieve their efficiency by an entire social context (wage structure, employment structure, consumer structure, all connected to the dominant division of labour in the factory) that is lacking in the USSR. One may well doubt whether these factories are organised for optimum performance and function properly.

But that is not all. By importing these plants, the USSR is continuing a policy which in certain ways resembles the attempts to solve the problem of underdevelopment within the capitalist system. This is the policy of the so-called development pole; it consists in establishing a large installation in an area to be developed, an installation with highly developed technology, which can initiate the development of the area or sector. But this does not always function according to the original hopes. In *Pravda* of 17 and 18 August 1971, two highly interesting articles appeared, dealing with the progress of work and the production of Fiat cars in the large factory at Togliattigrad.[51] The newspaper

reported on an internal meeting of the factory management which
ascertained that production had been too low from a qualitative
point of view and had provoked too many letters of protest from
consumers.[52] In part, the problem was caused by the poor co-ordination of different sub-contractors. But there were major problems
even inside the factory. Director Poliakov warned against shifting
one's own responsibility on to others. We grasp the sense of this
warning when we look at the many interviews which journalists
had with workers: libraries and cinemas are still lacking; the
worker does not know what to do in his free time, and this
obviously has negative results upon the subjective, human element
of productivity, leading to absenteeism and diminished co-operation.[53] Furthermore, it is not improbable that a part of the
dissatisfaction stems from the desire to impose Western work
rates upon the workers. This was certainly a necessary attempt if
there was to be optimum performance, but it was also condemned
to failure, for reasons already mentioned.

In Togliattigrad, the typical dysfunctions of the Soviet economic
structure are once again manifest. Here we can observe a quite
striking phenomenon. In capitalism, the development pole policy
produces what Celso Furtado, the well-known Brazilian economist,
has called the "tropical plant effect": the big plant functions like
those gigantic trees which spread their roots over the entire
ground, soaking up all the water and destroying the smaller trees
around them (the small enterprises). In the USSR, the converse
takes place: it is the sub-contracting plants which, because of
their own incapacity, ultimately impair the performance of large-
scale plans by supplying them with defective material.

This situation has far-reaching consequences for Soviet society.
The price of relations with the West is very high, and the fact that
the results of these relations have been negative strengthens
already existing social tensions. In particular, the proponents of
theories of the market economy can make use of these dysfunctions to demand a radical capitalisation of the economy (read: a
restoration of capitalism). In other words, they want a social
context for the large-scale factory and its ability to produce
results. Experiences such as those at Togliattigrad will sharpen
the social and political controversies in the country, because of the
deepening and unsolved economic contradictions.

On the basis of this ultimately negative balance, we should ask ourselves why the Soviet bureaucracy so desperately holds on to its political and economic coexistence with the West. The reason is simple: it has no alternative. In some cases, cyclical problems can be solved by means of economic relations with the West (we need only think of the grain sales of the 1960s), problems whose neglect could endanger the already politically tense situation within the country. A return to undiluted stalinism, i.e. to strong discipline with an economic barrier against the West, would not solve the structural contradictions, which result from organic dysfunctions. Moreover, excessive restraint would have no success at a time when the economy is becoming ever harder to control by means of planning. There are certain economic problems — at least the ones mentioned above — that cannot be solved by the secret police.

The bureaucracy sees itself compelled to oscillate between making concessions to the technocrats (e.g. the 1965 reforms) and rescinding them, while lacking the power to return, in its domestic and foreign policy, to the no longer practicable positions of the 1950s.[54]

In this mixture of oscillation in its domestic policy and weakness in its foreign policy towards the West, the historic crisis of the Soviet bureaucracy becomes clear. One question remains: can the crisis of capitalism, which many people (myself included) hold to be near, help the USSR? In my opinion, no. If the crisis breaks out, it will be one of over-production, as the American marxists of the group around *Monthly Review* (especially Sweezy and Magdoff) have already demonstrated. Such a crisis, which includes a saturation of the market, will certainly not make the "bad" Soviet commodities any more appetising; the limitation of production will result in a limitation of the demand for raw materials. To be sure, the West will have an even greater need to find outlets. But when you want to get rid of your commodities, you must first find a buyer, and this fails to fit the scenario above. At best the USSR will be able, as in 1929, to conclude a couple of good deals: but not more.

Conclusion: seven theses on the foreign policy of the Soviet Union

(1.) The Soviet policy of coexistence signifies a break with leninism.

(2.) The Soviet foreign policy of coexistence represents, in spite of the socio-political continuity which has existed since 1928, an innovation by comparison with stalinist foreign policy.

(3.) This policy is an attempt to counter the structural crisis of the system that was established under Stalin and perfected after his death.

(4.) As a result, this policy expresses the interest in survival of the new ruling class of the USSR.

(5.) The fact that there is no alternative to this policy from the bureaucracy's point of view makes it "inevitable", and explains the extreme caution of the Soviet leaders in their relations with the USA.

(6.) Trade with the West only brings the USSR cyclical, not structural advantages — in addition, it can even accelerate the internal crisis.

(7.) Nevertheless, the Soviet bureaucracy sees itself compelled to continue this policy, since it has no demonstrable alternative.

NOTES

1. A. Beliakov and F. Burlackij, "Die leninistische Theorie der sozialistischen Revolution unserer Zeit", in *Kommunist* 13 (September 1960).

2. W. I. Lenin, "Uber unsere Revolution", in *W. I. Lenin, Werke*, vol. 33 (Berlin 1971), p. 462-7.

3. I wish to emphasise that I disagree with the thesis that Russia was a feudal country, a notion which has been advanced by various exponents of the working-class movement (e.g. Gramsci). In spite of its globally lower stage of development, the tsarist empire had, in comparison with German, English or American development, taken many steps along the road to capitalism in the years before the revolution. Cf. A. Carlo, "La natura socio-economica dell'URSS", in *Giovane critica* 26, p. 75 ff.

4. The thesis of the USSR as a degenerate workers' state derives from the trotskyists. Already in the 1930s, a small minority were denying that the USSR had even this distorted proletarian character.

5. This seriously disturbed the USSR; cf. S. Pervouchine, "La nouvelle étape", in *Recherches internationales à la lumière du marxisme* 56, p. 7 ff. The approximation of the industrial rates of growth of the "socialist" and capitalist countries, which occurred at the beginning of the 1960s, dampened many of Khrushchev's ambitions, in particular that of rapidly overtaking the West.

6. Theoretically there exists an obvious analogy between the Soviet theories and the economism of the Second International; cf. U. Schmiederer, *Zur sowjetischen Theorie der friedlichen Koexistenz* (Frankfurt 1968), p. 70.

7. Cf. Carlo, "The Socio-Economic Nature of the USSR", in *Telos* 21 (1974).

8. These weaknesses existed before, but became even more intense with the development of the economy.

9. The existence of conflicts between the two superpowers should not give us the mistaken impression that the USSR is a socialist country. It is a country with an antagonistic but non-capitalist structure. If conflicts of interest between countries with the same antagonistic structures — in effect, capitalist countries — can arise, the same is even more true for countries with different antagonistic structures. Both of the superpowers have only tactical differences of opinion, since strategically they pursue the same goal: prevention of the socialist revolution, which would lead to the overthrow of all ruling classes, of the bourgeoisie as well as of the bureaucracy.

10. M. Gutelman ("La politica economica cubana", in *Il nuovo marxismo latinoamericano* [Milan 1970], p. 78 ff.) adopts a peculiar position: on the one hand he emphasises the effectiveness of Cuban policy, and on the other he justifies its strangulation by the Soviets. Considering the good relations between Gutelman and the Cubans, we cannot exclude the possibility that the latter requested him to make a public presentation of the facts without frontally attacking the Soviets.

11. A country affected by dumping can certainly fight back, since the legitimacy of dumping is generally recognised in international relations.

12. Cf. L. Huberman and P. Sweezy, *Socialism in Cuba* (New York 1969).

13. L. Maitan, Preface to L. D. Trotsky, *La terza internazionale dopo Lenin* (Milan 1957), p. 20. The parallels between détente (peaceful coexistence) and socialism in one country have been frequently drawn. In this case, I do not criticise Maitan, whose interpretation I find correct for the period 1934-39; but I assert the existence of radically different causes in the case of stalinist and post-stalinist foreign policy, which are only apparently similar — for example, in the case of the Popular Front.

14. In fact the total volume of trade in 1928 — according to the value of the ruble on 1 January 1961 — accounted for 1,377 million (1932: 1,033 m., 1937: 524 m., 1940: 1,280 m.) and in 1950, 2,925 million, i.e. little more than twice that of the year taken as comparison, 1928. The figures are taken from the collection *60 anni di statistiche dell'Unione Sovietica*, published in 1974 in Rome by the Associazione Italia-URSS. In 1950 there was almost no trade with the West, and it is certain that the idea of the secondary importance of foreign trade came into currency among Soviet economic officials in these years. This position was sharply criticised by Kosygin in 1966, since it had become outdated in the meantime and was detrimental to the economy.

15. For Stalin's extremism in the period 1928-34, cf. Trotsky, *The Third International after Lenin* (New York 1957).

16. My fairly radical critique of Rizzi provoked an ardent polemic between the former trotskyist and myself; cf. B. Rizzi, "Sulla natura dell'URSS; replicando a Giovane critica", in *Giovane critica* 28, p. 51 ff.; Carlo, "Sulla natura dell'URSS, Risposta a Rizzi e a Melotti", in *Terzo Mondo* 15, p. 74 ff.

17. We wish to once again emphasise that it is a question not only of favouring but of incurable favouring. In the industrial boom phase, e.g. in late tsarist Russia, or in a phase similar to it, e.g. the industrial reconstruction of postwar Japan, capitalist countries frequently exhibit a significant favouring (I would say of the "Soviet" kind) of the industrial primary sector. But over a period of time an essentially more balanced relationship establishes itself between the primary and the secondary sector, whose further development becomes predominant. In the USA in the period from 1879-1929, the primary sector increased thirteen times, the secondary seven times, while in the period between 1929 and 1962 the relation seemed to change: the primary sector increased twofold, the secondary by 2.68; cf. Pervouchine, p. 25. We can observe similar phenomena in Japan after the reconstruc-

tion, cf. Carlo, "Giappone: verso la fine del miracolo", in *Terzo Mondo* 15, p. 39 ff. The difference between the two systems thus lies in the incurability of the severe and anomalous incongruity in the Soviet Union between sector I and sector II.

18. Even in discussing capitalism, one speaks of a plan. The capitalist plan, unlike the Soviet one, does not set itself above the market and its principles but subordinates itself to them and has a different character: it is indicative and not compulsory. To reduce the Soviet plan to something resembling the capitalist one means completely overturning the relations of production.

19. Cf. section 6 and Carlo, "The Socio-Economic Nature" etc., p. 61 ff.

20. In 1970, the eighth five-year plan (1966-70) also failed in various branches of sector I, which make up the main branches of Soviet planning. Here are some representative figures for production in 1970: electrical energy 740 billion Kwh (830-50 planned); gas 200 billion cubic metres (225-40 planned); coal 624 million tons (665-75 planned); chemical fertilisers, at least 10% or less than planned; cement 95.2 million tons (100-105 planned); steel 116 million tons (124-29 planned); textiles 8.7 billion square metres (9.5-9.8 planned).

21. A. Kosygin and L. Brezhnev, *Bericht zum XXIII Kongress der KPdSU*, Rome 1966, p. 159 c.

22. Cf. Kosygin, *Der Fünfjahresplan der UdSSR 1971-1975*, Rome 1971, p. 73.

23. I have taken the figures on foreign trade for this chapter from the collection *60 anni di statistiche dell'Unione Sovietica*, as well as from a publication of the Banca Commerciale Italiana (*Il portolano del mondo economico: paesi socialisti*, Rome 1972).

24. The underdeveloped countries must be generally regarded as capitalist ("peripheral" capitalism), as has been sufficiently demonstrated in the meantime; only in some of these countries (e.g. the United Arab Republic under Nasser) can one speak of specific forms of bureaucratic collectivism, cf. Carlo, "The Socio-Economic Nature" etc., p. 71 ff.

25. It should be noted that the Soviet balance of payments is very often passive in relation to the neocapitalist countries, while it is active or in equilibrium as a whole. In 1970, for example, imports from highly developed countries were 2.5 billion rubles, while export only amounted to 2.2 billion rubles.

26. Kosygin's report of 1966 emphasises the necessity of giving priority to the development of the export sector. The Soviet

Vice-Minister for Foreign Trade, N. N. Smelyakov, had to admit in 1973 in an article in *Novy mir*, 2, that the situation of the sector is very unsatisfactory.

27. In 1960, machine exports to the West accounted for 9.6% of the total exports of the sector in question, but in 1970 for only 3%; the change is too insignificant to permit one to speak of a trend.

28. Cf. note 26.

29. Cf. *Unitá*, 30 June 1974.

30. The figures can be grouped as follows: petroleum and petroleum derivatives 90.967 billion lire, minerals and scrap 34.688 billion lire.

31. In 1970, the East German trade deficit amounted to 373 million marks (1969: 419 m., 1964: 234 m.), while in 1961 the balance was active to the extent of 66 million. In 1970, trade between East and West Germany accounted for 10.2% of the total trade of East Germany and only 1.9% of the foreign trade of West Germany. Taken as a whole, East Germany shows a greater proclivity to foreign trade than the USSR; this can be explained by the fact that East Germany produces products of better quality. Nevertheless, East Germany lags far behind capitalist countries in this area; one not infrequently observes signs of concern about this lag in the East German press. In the East European countries, there exists a broad spectrum of varying quality in the level of production, although the structural characteristics are all the same. Development also does not occur identically in the different countries of bureaucratic collectivism. After the reforms of 1965 a scale of East European countries became evident, at one end of which stands the USSR, where the reforms were very limited and modest in their practical execution, and at the other end Yugoslavia, where capitalism was restored by means of the reforms (cf. Carlo, "L'esperienza jugoslava: dal colletivismo burocratico alla restaurazione del capitalismo", in *Terzo mondo* 18, p. 47 ff.); in between lie different countries with a bureaucratic collectivism "tainted" by the reforms of 1965 and the introduction of marketing principles — the same, however, is not true of Albania, about which I have not yet arrived at a final assessment.

32. Cf. Smelyakov, p. 871, who strongly criticises the policy of the Bank of Foreign Trade.

33. It is symptomatic that Czechoslovakia's balance of trade with the neocapitalist countries frequently shows a deficit. In 1970, Czechoslovakia's exports to highly developed capitalist countries

amounted to roughly 5.5 billion kroner (20% of total exports), while imports accounted for 6.6 billion kroner (25% of total imports).

34. Cf. *Il portolano*, p. 61, note 134.

35. It is therefore illuminating that the Soviets thought the risk of Czechoslovakia's entering the Western sphere and breaking away from Comecon to be so great. This risk, along with the necessity of stopping the technocratic reform process, must have moved the USSR to intervention.

36. Cf. Carlo, "The Socio-Economic Nature" etc., p. 82 ff.

37. A structure similar to that of trade relations with Czechoslovakia also characterises relations with East Germany.

38. The Italian trade partners are well acquainted with the ponderousness and complexity of Soviet planning (cf. R. Roncaglia in *Quaderni del Politico* 3 (1966), p. 183 ff.). But the former strike a far more modest tone in their critique than do certain Soviet representatives of industry, who have expressed themselves much more sharply (cf., for example, O. Antonov, *La pianificazione sovietica* [Florence 1968]).

39. Cf. Kosygin, *Der Fünfjahresplan* etc., p. 19 ff., cf. also Carlo, "The Socio-Economic Nature" etc., p. 102 ff.

40. Smelyakov, p. 884.

41. Ibid., p. 885.

42. Ibid. It should be noted that the Vice-Minister emphasises the progress of the USSR, as well as Western libels upon Soviet production, several times in his article. Nevertheless, in the passages cited here, the true causes for the Soviet lag in the area of plant export are quite evident:

> "Unfortunately, the export of machines, plant and replacement parts has been viewed by some factories until recently as a form of punishment. Actually, the demands which the client has to make upon production create no concern in such areas as the technical-economic level, quality, aesthetics, promptness of delivery, the satisfaction of the buyer, special features (for which he pays), the organisation of technical assistance for the lifespan of the machinery, packing and transport. . . . It is quite difficult to find a factory director who would propose an additional delivery of automobiles, tractors, metal-cutting machines or other machine tools for export" (p. 874).

43. The same is also true for those semi-manufactured products whose production does not require any particularly skilled labour.

44. See also section 4.
45. Cf. P. Jalée, "La corsa alle materie prime", in *Rinascita*, 6 (1974), p. 15 ff.
46. After Gunder Frank, in *Il Manifesto*, 29 March 1972.
47. One should not be deceived by the positive outcome of the economic plan for 1973. As well-known experts who have close ties with the USSR admit, the strategic problems which are decisive for the success of the five-year plan have not been even initially solved. Sector II of industry failed to overtake the growth rate of sector I. This means that consumption and wages have not risen as hoped for — with the result that popular dissatisfaction will continue to have an effect upon the low level of labour productivity. The boom is merely cyclical, the structural problems remain unsolved.
48. The cautious foreign policy of the USSR has been criticised by its sympathisers — see the report of Manuel Ascarate to the Central Committee of the Spanish Communist Party for September 1973, which was sharply answered from the Russian side; cf. *Monthly Review* 3 (1974), p. 21 ff.
49. Cf. Carlo, "The Socio-Economic Nature" etc., p. 78, note 217.
50. Ibid., p. 24 ff., note 76.
51. Cf. *Quaderni Ceses* (1971), p. 1411 ff.
52. The passage from the speech of the official responsible, reproduced in the article, reads: "Comrades . . . , yesterday and the day before we were not able to keep to the programme, we have not reached the norm of 600 automobiles a day. Production in the paint-shop was of inferior quality; there were faults in the welding. Our work has caused too many letters of protest because of the bad quality of production."
53. Cf. *Quaderni Ceses*, p. 1418 ff.
54. Even the repression was quite mild in comparison to Stalin's time. Dubcek was replaced with a moderate like Husak.

5

Social structure and foreign policy
in the Soviet Union

RAINER ROTERMUNDT &
URSULA SCHMIEDERER

Preliminary remarks

Since the end of the "Cold War", scientific discussion has once
again turned to a problem that seemed to have been solved at the
time: the problem of the mode of social functioning of the non-
capitalist countries, and in particular of the Soviet Union, as the
historical and political centre of the "socialist camp" that is not
oriented to the Chinese model. Today, for example, we have seen
a resumption of the tradition of left oppositional and trotskyist
analyses from the period before the Second World War.[1] In addition, the attempt to conceive the social relationships of socialist
countries as "statist", familiar from the Yugoslavian discussion,
has recently played a significant role.[2] The newer approaches of
Hillel Ticktin and Antonio Carlo cannot be assigned to any of
these categories. In the following pages, we intend to examine the
range of these theories in order to formulate certain theses dealing
with the question of the relation between social structure and
foreign policy in the Soviet Union, none of which, however,
coincide with the above-mentioned hypotheses.[3]

Soviet bureaucracy and social relations from Hillel Ticktin's point of view

Unlike Charles Bettelheim, Paul Sweezy or Serge Mallet, Ticktin
describes the social structure of the Soviet Union as being neither
(state) capitalist nor actually socialist.[4] He seeks a positive definition on the one hand in the phenomenon of the bureaucracy and
on the other, in the enormous waste of social resources.[5]

The continuing existence of the bureaucracy, explained in the first place by the contradiction between planning and the market which made itself felt after the October revolution, goes almost without saying for Ticktin. He describes it as an institutionalised instrument of struggle against opposition in any form, with industrialisation in the end turning into a conscious act for the consolidation of power.[6] Moreover, Ticktin fails to live up to his own analytical claim of accounting for the bureaucracy by means of the social structure, when he traces the longevity of the Soviet state back to the activities of the secret police.[7] He also explains some of the political and economic aspirations of part of the intelligentsia by referring them ultimately to the individuals themselves, by attributing to them a lust for money or an uncritical imitation of Western "models", without making any attempt to derive their structures of consciousness from their position in the process of social reproduction.

Ticktin deals with his second basic phenomenon, the waste of social resources, in a similar fashion. He describes it in its various manifest forms (low quality of products, reluctance to introduce new technology, underemployment, insufficient utilisation of available capacity)[8] and offers the explanation that, on the one hand, the central planning authority has too little information at its disposal to be able to plan precisely and that, on the other hand, the factory directors are concerned only with their own prosperity. But one can hardly be satisfied with such an explanation, unless one is willing to ascribe momentarily contrary interests to the planners (or executive organs, as the case may be) in and of themselves, in their capacity as human individuals. Rather, by its very existence, this opposition points to a relation between planning and execution which contradicts the socialist claim;[9] in a society whose members consciously plan their lives (and *are able* to plan), one might encounter certain "frictional losses" in the course of putting the plan into practice, but any essential divergence between "above" and "below", between planners and planned, would be excluded: i.e. this difference would not be a social but a technical one. The simple fact that one part of Soviet society plans *for* another, in its place, enables one to deduce the existence of structural difficulties.

At this point Ticktin picks up the notion of an "atomised"

society. He offers no explanation of how it functions, but simply makes use of this category in order to shift the conflict of interests to the foreground of his argument, a procedure which finally results in a vicious circle: atomisation is viewed as a presupposition *and* a result of the functioning of the bureaucracy's repressive mechanisms — the bureaucracy consequently explains its own existence.[10]

Parallel to this line of argument there runs a second one, in which the bureaucracy appears as the mere administrator of objective laws, as the exact opposite of the planning tyrant. Ticktin speaks about an organised economy, one whose organisers cannot essentially control, but which follows its own immanent laws.[11] Ticktin fails to arrive at a mediation between these mutually contradictory propositions. We may suppose that he would refer this latter difficulty once again to the conflict between planning and private interests (those of the factory directors as well as the workers),[12] which would still lead him into a blind alley: without recourse to the structural contradiction, he would once again find himself involved in the same vicious circle, which would then only be able to support itself by falling back upon anthropological constants or upon organisational (or sociological) compulsion. One can in no way speak of a solution to the problem.

Apart from the foregoing, we can distinguish some additional theoretical inconsistencies. We have to agree with Ticktin when he asserts that the living standards of the Soviet worker depend upon the quantity of money which he receives as a "wage". Nevertheless, it remains questionable whether one can compare this situation to the sale of his labour power as a commodity, as Ticktin supposes.[13] To say of a system of social relations that within its framework human labour power changes into a commodity can only mean that this society is a capitalist one. But one must consequently thus see a new bourgeoisie in the Soviet bureaucracy, which Ticktin explicitly refuses to do.[14] He goes so far as to deny any class character to the bureaucracy;[15] its social function thus becomes completely incomprehensible, especially since Ticktin's argument — that the high personal permeability and internal antagonisms of the factional interests enable us to speak only of an élite — will not stand up. In the long run, one's decision to view a portion of the society as a class depends upon its position in the context of the reproduction of society as a whole, and not upon the uniformity of its members (although in specific cases the two may fuse together). Even a divergence of interests within a class does not necessarily call its class status in question; antagonistic factions of capital are, for example, inseparable from the existence of the bourgeoisie as a class. Once more, Ticktin ends up explaining the bureaucracy by means of itself, and this will inevitably continue to be the case as long as there is no recognition of its objective function within the context of the reproduction of societies of the Soviet type.

Antonio Carlo and the problem of the bureaucracy

Carlo's projected solution leads to the same difficulty, in so far as it likewise fails to "find the concept" of the bureaucracy. Carlo shares Ticktin's general evaluation of the neither-capitalist-nor-socialist character of the Soviet Union,[16] but he considers the bureaucracy to be a class in its own right: "Actually, ownership of the means of production (understood as the power to dispose of them for one's interest outside of any veto and control) in Russia belongs to the bureaucracy considered collectively as a class."[17]

Naturally, for Carlo the bureaucratic power of disposition cannot be identical with private property, since this would mean that Soviet society is just a modification of the capitalist one. But he is therefore confronted with the question, what function does the bureaucracy actually have? And more particularly, how is one to recognise the pressures which make themselves felt behind its back as well as the form in which those pressures are socially transmitted? But the basic assessment of Soviet society as a non-capitalist one prevents one from falling back upon the law of value.

Carlo points to the "need to conquer backwardness", as well as the "antagonisms with capitalist countries",[18] as determinants in the decision-making of the dominant class. But the Chinese example illustrates how the latter explanation often falls short of the mark. We must not overlook the limitations on the possibilities of socialist development in relation to conflict with the capitalist West; but this negative definition in no way implies the objective necessity of social structures of the Soviet type. The

concept of backwardness eliminates any socially qualitative determination and reduces the Soviet Union's relation with the West
to a technical category. In the same way, many Kremlinologists
have reduced it to the level of a geographical (East-West) or
anthropological category (the "essence" of "Soviet man"). Nevertheless, a "technological gap" does not imply the existence of
economic pressure "to keep up with" or even "to overtake". This
pressure only arises under given international and social pre-
suppositions, such as that "highly developed" and "less developed" countries act as technological competitors on the world
market (i.e. under the presupposition that one is dealing with
capitalist countries on both sides). Behind the technical, quantitative difference there appears its qualitative basis: the different
degrees of development of the production of relative surplus
value, and thus the different stages of a *capitalist* mode of production. Where the relations of production are qualitatively
unequal, this kind of comparison (frequently employed in studies
about the USA and the Soviet Union) loses its affirmative power,
in fact it obscures the important problems.[19]

The following question must be asked. To what extent does
this specific situation of the Soviet Union — that of not being
able to escape from the world market and of having at least to
act as a buyer and seller there — operate within the country
itself? That is to say, what contradictions arise between the
socialist claim to social transformation (including that of direct
working conditions) and the pressure to produce at a "world
market level" (at least in branches of the export industry), i.e. to
apply technology which in essence cannot be separated from its
function of extorting surplus value?

The original problem is therefore altered, as follows. We have
to ask ourselves why and how such pressures against the socialist
claim exist, and, furthermore, how anyone can fail to see that such
inhibiting factors act as obstacles, with the result that Soviet
science conceives "backwardness" in the same commonplace
manner as bourgeois statistics and the slogan "catch up with and
overtake" can seem to point in the direction of socialism.[20]

Wherever it is that one might discover the "silent pressure"
of social relations in a concrete case — in the sense that "the
bureaucratic apparatus dominates production by running it in

its own interests"[21] — in any case one certainly cannot say. At all events, it could be an inversion by which the bureaucrats perceive the interests imposed upon them as an objective force, as being their "own" — this would be analogous to the way that capital strives to realise itself and enforces itself beyond the subjective actions of the bourgeoisie.

Carlo thus arrives at the crossroads of the problem of the bureaucracy. Either one can stop at the "peculiar" interests of the bureaucracy, which in the end remain unexplained, or one has to extend the inquiry, to ask how the bureaucracy's forms of behaviour are mediated by the underlying productive relations, to ask how the bureaucracy becomes the executive organ, what objective pressures it has to deal with, what alternatives result from them, and in what "inverted" form its own self-image is fashioned.

Relations of production in the Soviet Union : an attempt at a concrete definition

If one agrees with the assessment that the Soviet Union is a non-capitalist *and* non-socialist society, this means that the category of commodities does not determine, or perhaps no longer determines, the "elementary form" of that society, although its existence in certain areas cannot be denied. The problem arises of how a mode of production can come into existence in which there is the formation of value (commodity production) but not the realisation of capital, and in which commodity production is therefore no longer socially generalised. In this connection, two further questions arise. First of all, how is the industrial labour process determined and what are the consequences of the fact that the producers earn money "for" their labour? Without the process of realisation one can naturally speak neither of the commodity value nor of the sale of labour power. And secondly, what objective function does commodity production have in the framework of the overall process of social reproduction?[22]

In answer to the second question, one must agree with Mandel's conclusion (in spite of his shaky reasoning) when he observes that "the mass of the big means of production in industry, transport, communications, trade, etc. has no commodity character."[23] But there follows an unclear division:

"The consumer goods industrially produced according to the plan have a commodity form only inasmuch as they are produced for an anonymous market and must be exchanged against money. They do not have that form in the sense that they are products of private labour."[24]

If certain things must be produced for an anonymous market (as Mandel himself admits, which can only mean that they cannot be distributed in any other way), and must subsequently establish their social character — whether intended by the plan or not — by realising their value, one cannot interpret this otherwise than as the result of private production (at least as a foundation, which possibly encroaches upon other areas, by imposing a commodity character upon non-privately produced articles).

At all events, we have still said nothing about the importance of private production. Confronted with the alternative which Mandel seems to see between commodity production and planning (the production of use values), one must carefully differentiate between generalised and marginal commodity production in society as a whole. If we do not consider the Soviet Union to be a simple modification of capitalist relations but nevertheless assume the existence of commodity categories in certain areas, then the question arises: what are the causes of the continuing existence of private production, as well as its mediation by the determining factors — the "inner bond" — of Soviet-type societies?

We could perhaps clarify this latter point by pointing to the analogy between commodity production and feudal social structure. In its essential traits, feudalism is not a mode of production based upon private labour, but the concept of feudalism implies the marginal existence of such labour, otherwise it would not be historically conceivable. One can find a similar situation in the relationship between city and country in so-called "underdeveloped" regions (for example, in Latin America); but here one needs a concept of the structures which would illuminate the immanent reciprocity of both sides.[25]

To do this in the case of the Soviet Union means offering a real explanation for the survival of commodity production (in contrast to the socialist demand for its gradual elimination).

Mandel oversimplifies his case by falling back upon the scarcity of basic necessities and upon the low level of development of the means of production.[26] In agreement with Soviet economists, he thus encourages the beautiful illusion that commodity production would completely vanish with the development of the means of production; this is a striking legitimation of the stalinist model of industrialisation by its trotskyist critic, and it rests upon an incorrect appreciation of what commodity production means. The various historical forms of non-capitalist society, from the Incas down to the present-day Chinese, demonstrate one thing: that mere scarcity in no way stimulates the development of the commodity form, but rather the "social action" of human beings against the background of given socio-historic preconditions. If one explains commodity production on the basis of scarcity, one not only grants it a natural character, but one also reduces the problem of eliminating it to a purely technical one.

In Mandel's argument, we can clearly see a general characteristic of discussions about the nature of Soviet society: the producers appear to both "left" and "right" wing critics rather as the objects of the existing relations (or as objects postulated for the sake of improving their lives) than as their real creators and agents; the producers become the victims of charitable and pedagogical drives. One attempts to describe and conceive society "from above", as it were; critics scratch their heads over the bureaucracy, and the not entirely accidental result is that they pursue sociological inquiries about whether the bureaucracy is an élite, or even a class, instead of attempting to determine its objective social function. In this regard, neither the social origins of the bureaucrats nor differences in accounting methods can help, nor can they ever answer the questions about the situation of the producers in the process of production and reproduction.[27] One completely loses sight of the fact that the basic problem of socialism does not lie in a reciprocal relation between "butter or guns" (Carlo), i.e. between sector I and sector II, but in the elimination of the bureaucracy, which only the producers themselves can achieve.

In taking up the question of the productive relations, we must be careful about employing the term "wage labour" when realisation of capital does not take place, since labour power does not become a commodity as it does under capitalism. Nevertheless, the producers do not simply receive use values which are distributed according to their needs and according to their own plan, and which are only limited by the extent of natural resources; they receive money, whose quantity limits their opportunities for satisfying their needs. This means that the reproduction of the producers is mediated by the exchange of commodities, although the exchange relation in the case of individual commodities need not necessarily directly express the magnitude of their value, since the planning authority maintains certain limits on the price of consumer goods.[28] One has to ask how these limits are determined. To be sure, the law of value is only completely effective under conditions of socially generalised commodity production, but "simple" commodity production already imposes certain limits upon the efforts of the planners.[29] How one answers this question depends upon the objective mediation between marginal commodity production and the basic social mechanism from which commodity production receives its marginal character.

The decisive question is: how does it happen that the products are not only alienated from the producers (although they are not privately appropriated by the bureaucrats) by taking on a commodity form, but that the producers also have no power over their instruments of production, so that workers find themselves forced to adopt passive forms of resistance which are expressed in a low level of productivity?[30]

Although it does not own private property, the bureaucracy decides about both the objects and the means of production. Its decisions are modified because of its non-capitalist relation to the producer: to the extent that the producers do not determine their own destiny and neither they nor the bureaucracy are constrained by the realisation of capital, bureaucratic decisions remain completely external to the relations of production. It is thus possible to shift the relative loads about between sector I and sector II; *both* together, however, no more bring the Soviet Union closer to socialism than would the shift of a capitalist pharmaceutical concern from the manufacture of morphine to that of oral contraceptives.

Measures would assume a socialist character if they were aimed at eliminating the bureaucracy instead of reorienting it. To discover the conditions under which this could take place, one would need to analyse the social function of the Soviet bureaucracy. In this sense, we must differentiate between two aspects: an external one and an internal one. The external one stems from the Soviet Union's participation in a capitalist world market in the form of foreign trade and international exchange. Since the world market obeys the laws of value, which expresses itself in the international competition of capital, the USSR finds itself compelled (it wants to participate in exchange without being exposed to the possibility of a permanent disadvantageous transfer of value) to offer and consequently to produce its commodities according to the standards of the world market. Since these standards have not developed under the USSR's conditions of production, with its lack of a need for realisation of capital, the bureaucracy must implement these standards at the expense of the producers. In this way, the bureaucrats end up imitating the actual character traits of capital — and, of course, all in the name of socialism (a legitimation of authority which can be perceived not as cynicism but as objective functionality, although not as ideology in a marxist sense).

The authority exercised as such in the Soviet Union has for a long time ceased to possess the mediated character it possesses in bourgeois states. This means that the separation of power and authority, of state and society, is different in the USSR, if we consider the unmediated form in which the bureaucracy, as the incarnation of the state, avails itself of the social function of authority. Unlike the bourgeois state, it fulfils no objective general interest of capital in relation to its own concretions (that is to say, it is not an *ideal* aggregate capitalist), but rather the interest of the producers, although it does so by putting pressure upon them (i.e. *real* socialist substitutionism). The cause of this does not lie in some kind of naturally given opposition between the interests of the producers and those of the bureaucracy (cf. Ticktin above), but in the fact that under the given circumstances of the alienation of the producers from their own conditions of production, on the one hand their interests can only be exercised in this perverted form; and on the other hand, for this very reason, the producers only pursue and formulate interests which superficially resemble those of the consumers of bourgeois society, although they have a completely different origin.

We have finally arrived at the internal causes of the bureaucracy, and of the bureaucratic state as the result and guarantee of the social disenfranchisement of a once revolutionary working class.[31] The question now arises of how such social structures could have developed from the Russian revolution, what objective character the revolution possessed (apart from its own goals) and what social pressures have caused it so far to resist the elimination of alienated labour.

We have already stated, with regard to the latter question, that from a truly socialist perspective the elimination of the bureaucratic alternative between butter or guns can only be achieved by the producers themselves. But because of their social powerlessness, they direct themselves precisely to much-abused "private interests" — not because they are manipulated by Western "models" or because they are simply unenlightened as a result of the political "errors" of the bureaucracy, but because of social conditions which produce the opposition between bureaucracy and producers and have reproduced them up to the present time. In the forthcoming stage, the bureaucracy faces the dilemma of only being able to exercise its socialist substitutionism by appealing to anti-socialist structures of consciousness, since one cannot maintain the state of alienation without a minimum of social co-operation on the part of the producers, whose willingness to co-operate however is permanetly undercut by this same state of affairs and is pushed into a privatistic direction. This is what accounts for all those campaigns for raising production on the basis of appeals; as the alternative to direct, "material" stimuli, they are a call to the producers to combat the decay of socialism, to overcome their inner sluggishness (which is only there in the first place because such an appeal has become necessary). The bureaucrats go around in circles — and the workers feel the effects. To put it in more polemical terms, we could say that in the Soviet Union there is not a deformed workers' state but a state, or society, of deformed workers.[32]

For the bureaucracy, its kind of planning seems all the more necessary, the more passively the producers behave. And the more alienated the planning becomes, the more passive and privatised the behaviour of the producers.[33] The paradox is precisely that

there is neither a development towards capitalism nor towards
socialism, that Soviet society is characterised by fundamental
contradictions which give it a dynamic in no way comparable to
that of the drive for realisation of capital; the result is that
changes of direction (or spirals of development towards higher
levels of stagnation) essentially stem either from external shocks
in its relations with capitalist countries or from partial collabora-
tion with the latter, which requires changes for the sake of maintaining the system as a whole.

The vicious circle creates the impression that even to formulate
a socialist claim against the bureaucracy would be counter-
revolutionary. Theories of the bureaucracy presuppose that
socialism can be identified with the development of "productive
forces". This is a notion which both in itself and in the form of
a reduction of the concept of productive forces to that of tech-
nique, owes its existence to the alienation of the producers. That
is to say, as long as one leaves productive conditions unchallenged,
an advance in productive forces can only mean a further development of supposedly "neutral" social techniques (cf. the "scientific
and technological revolution"), with all its consequences for the
concept of socialism. It follows that each individual "labourer"
has the task of collaborating actively. Even all the forms of works
council at plant level (cf. the production committees in East Germany) have to dedicate themselves resolutely to the goal of what
in bureaucratic language is called "increased efficiency" and in the
workers' words is called "more drudgery". A demand for socialist
change in the conditions of production would be opposed to the
goal of "efficiency" and would lay itself open to the accusation
of being at the best uninformed and at the worst counter-revolutionary, and would be "rightly" subject to state repression. Here
the bureaucracy has, in its own mind, a thoroughly justified
legitimation for the touchy and often brutal way it reacts even
(or especially) to "leftist" attacks upon its position. An additional
paradox consists in the fact that a society whose declared aim is
to increase the productive forces by means of a continuing higher
development of technology cannot, because of the internal conditions which have given rise to this demand, make good the
claim. Since on the one hand there exists no effective power
behind the backs of the producers to further the development of

the productive forces, and since on the other hand the producers possess no power over these forces, we can generally assume that the Soviet Union relies crucially upon the import of capitalist technology.

The world market and foreign policy : the international conditions

The economic problems of the Soviet Union require an intensified turn towards the West and the import of capitalist technology, since at the same time their solution guarantees the stability of Soviet society as a whole. The Soviet interest in participating in the world market and the international division of labour, as well as in coexistence and détente, can be logically explained from these internal pressures. Carlo, like Ticktin, assumes that the need to import capitalist technology actually exists and will become stronger once the failures of the economic reforms have shown themselves, but also that the economic and social problems of Soviet society cannot be solved by means of such reforms and that the bottlenecks in the production and consumer goods industries and in agriculture will reproduce themselves anew.[34] According to Carlo and Ticktin, the function of détente and peaceful coexistence is to provide a support, from the angle of foreign policy, for economic endeavours.

If one deduces political and economic foreign relations so narrowly (in fact, almost exclusively) from internal conditions, one should at least deal with the problem that economic difficulties have always plagued the history of Soviet society. We thus need a special reason for the new turn towards détente. On the one hand, Carlo believes that the peaceful coexistence policy serves as an ideological disguise for the class interests of Soviet rulers as they develop their trade with capitalist countries;[35] the coexistence policy thus becomes a manipulative instrument that is employed consciously. On the other hand, a similarly tactical reading of Soviet foreign policy also emerges when Carlo distinguishes between the behaviour of Stalin and Khrushchev in questions of foreign policy. To be sure, the ever-present concern has been the preservation of Soviet society, the promotion of its economic development and its external security (which Carlo rightly calls a triviality, since this is true of the foreign policy of any nation-state); but in the Stalin period foreign policy was more strongly and "immediately political", while later on economic conditions became directly evident. Stalin proceeded in a much more flexible manner, and Carlo emphasises the contrast between his "high degree of flexibility", with its peculiar oscillations in governmental foreign policy and in the policy of the Communist International ("social fascism", the Popular Front, the Hitler-Stalin-Pact, etc.), and the subsequently more sharply limited range of possibilities which compel the current Soviet régime to make concessions or to desist and thus superficially impart a certain stability to the country's foreign policy.

Ticktin points out that the Soviet Union has imported capitalist technology since the 1920s.[37] From his point of view, the reason for the new turn towards the capitalist world market (as well as for the introduction of market forms inside the country) lies in the fact that the system has consumed its own historical foundations, and that today economic relations with the West have assumed quite a different urgency and inevitability.[38] The close fusion between economic reforms (as an expression of recently accumulated economic and social difficulties) and détente and coexistence still leave certain questions open. Viewed in this way, the policy is new, is due almost exclusively to internal conditions, and expresses an economic pressure for the turn towards the capitalist world market that has only now developed. But the longing gaze at the world market and the desire to take part in it is much older: Lenin's policy of concessions in the NEP was an attempt to gain admission to the capitalist world market and to attract capitalists, with their developed technology, into the country's producer goods sector. Even the supposed "autarky" of the Soviet state during the period of forced industrialisation and the first five-year plan was relative. After all, almost half of the total imports of the Soviet Union during the first five-year plan consisted of machines and equipment.[39] Although trade as a whole was quantitatively low, its role was to acquire "strategically" important goods for the industrialisation and construction of the Soviet Union.[40] Moreover, in Carlo's and Ticktin's interpretations, there is still the contradiction that they see economic problems as fundamentally entrenched in Soviet society. But these problems extend into the historical past, and one cannot offer such a neat explanation of the relation between the coexistence policy and recent economic reforms.

The more fundamental problem involves the use of certain models to explain foreign policy and the question of how far they can be applied to "socialist" foreign policy. Carlo and Ticktin start from the assumption that economics determines politics. They think that owing to this superiority of economics to politics, certain laws make themselves felt to which political strategies are subordinated. That is to say, in the case of the Soviet Union one cannot speak of a socialist society, since in such a society the "primacy of politics" would rate as the conscious and determining mode of action of the associated individuals. If economic laws make themselves felt, however, then there exist certain pressures on foreign policy to which politics is subject. But this would mean that the rulers cannot (as Carlo supposes) pursue a policy of coexistence or any other policy according to their wishes.

On the other hand, Carlo and Ticktin assert a "primacy" of domestic policy, and interpret foreign policy as secondary and derivative: it is a continuation of domestic policy abroad, in the interests of the dominant class or clique. In the case of bourgeois capitalist society, this is a quite usual way of explaining things. This would mean either that one is starting yet again from the assumption that such an interpretation is unproblematical, since the Soviet Union is no socialist society, or that it is an untested analytical model, which has yet to be problematised.

National foreign policy is fundamentally bound up with the rise of the bourgeois state, and thus with a political form which stamps intergovernmental relations as well as international politics in general with a specific content. This kind of national foreign policy presupposes the existence of a territorial state; the absolutist state, however, which created this precondition by monopolising central power and calling up a standing army, pursued a "transnational" policy, and its "dynastic interests, disguised as *raison d'état*," depended from the beginning upon a kind of aristocratic "international".[41] Along with the consensus of the aristocratic "international" there arose specific forms of intercourse. The European nobility formed a "transnational society", and the servants at princely courts or in the absolutist state reflected this fact.[42] The rise of bourgeois society and the development of the capitalist mode of production demanded for the first time a political form in which the dominant class could make its common interests felt both internally and externally.

The state has thus acquired a special existence alongside and external to bourgeois society, while at the same time it is the general political form of national capital. Owing to this peculiarity of its existence, and because it represents society as a whole, the state can represent a "national interest"; it can represent the "common good" of society abroad, and do so as a unit. Thus there exists a certain relationship between domestic and foreign policy. Up to the present time, governmental foreign policy has belonged to those *arcana imperii* which, even in bourgeois parliamentary terms, elude effective democratisation, being set apart from the affairs of society and isolated from them. Like national defence, foreign policy largely escapes the control of legislative decision-making processes (the same holds true for diplomacy and the practice of secret treaties). Certain functions of foreign policy therefore come into existence which are tied to the bourgeois national state: the security of its borders and territorial integrity, the security of the activities of citizens and organisations outside its borders, the creation of favourable conditions for its own social development, the preservation of society and thus partici- pation in international politics.

When a socialist society is obliged to take the form of a national state, this particular political form has certain conse- quences for the development of society as well as for its foreign relations. The continuing existence of this state as a general political form separated from society leads to internal relations of power and authority and creates the conditions for particular institutions (such as the military) which still exhibit traits of the bourgeois institution of the state, properly speaking. From the point of view of foreign policy, we can find no functions for this socialist state other than those we could itemise for the bourgeois state. The attempt to pursue a "socialist" national foreign policy involves an inherent contradiction. As long as the surrounding world and international politics are determined by the capitalist world market and its governmental forms of foreign policy, a socialist society can choose no political form of general representation other than that of the state; the choice is dictated by international conditions.[43] Therefore the state cannot "wither away", and a new "political form" which would have the task of eliminating the existing division between state and society fails to develop. It thus makes no sense to speak of the "neutrality" of the state, since it includes in and of itself structures of authority and power which must impair the development of socialist potential. For as long as capitalist society possesses, in the state, the political form for generalising and implementing the realisation of capital, and for as long as the capitalist mode of production continues its process of internationalisation, its production of a world market, and strives to integrate peoples and countries in its system of laws, then a socialist society will have no other choice than either to constitute itself politically in the form of a state or to pursue a foreign policy that is not a governmental one, thereby revealing the birthmarks of the old, capitalist society in a quite striking fashion.

A definition of "socialist" foreign policy simply on the basis of its social, "internal" conditions must fall short of the mark and overlook certain pre-existing international pressures. This is true for the character of governmental foreign policy and for relations with the capitalist world market. Governmental foreign policy must adapt itself to international conditions; it must operate with concessions and compromises. The charge that Soviet foreign policy is not revolutionary is rather a moralistic one, which, strictly speaking, is directed towards abandoning governmental foreign policy and putting revolutionary class politics in its place.[44] The Soviet Union has always had difficulties in presenting its foreign policy as a "socialist" one, because no such a thing as a "socialist foreign policy" can exist. According to its internal conditions, socialist foreign policy would not be determined by the executive, the state or the government, but formulated within the society by the producers — a situation which has never existed in the Soviet Union. In addition, socialist foreign policy could only consist of revolutionary class politics, which would transcend existing forms of international relations and necessarily threaten the governmental existence of socialist society (not only the Soviet but likewise the Chinese, the North Korean and Vietnamese societies). In a subsequent stage it would necessarily lead to a dismantling of repressive institutions such as the military and to a weakening of the bureaucracy, which both internally and externally appears as the representative and bearer of a "socialist national interest", thereby securing its own position beyond the reach of any social control. But the state would then no longer be a state at all.

Carlo and Ticktin expressly emphasise one dimension of the USSR's dependency upon the capitalist world market.[45] Along with production plants, it also imports the capitalist organisation of labour and factories, wage systems, techniques, management methods etc. The productive forces of living labour are subject to conditions set by the capitalist mode of production. The relationship with the world market is supposed to help overcome economic bottlenecks and to serve as a means of increasing the productive forces. If the development of productive forces rates as a goal with high social priorities in itself, as it does in the Soviet Union, it makes sense to turn to the capitalist world market, since the capitalist mode of production has achieved an increase in productive forces to a revolutionary degree and with a higher dynamic.

But participation in the world market has other dimensions too. On the one hand, if a constant transfer of value is not to take place, one must produce at its own level and be able to withstand its capacity for competition. Production for export must not only direct its output towards successful competition, it must also let itself be guided by demand within the world market. But the competitive situation on the world market leads to a constant change of marketing possibilities and presupposes a high flexibility in export production on the part of Soviet industry. This part of production thus tends to evade the conditions of planning, since the need to make constant and quick changes interferes with development according to the plan. Here, then, are additional considerations for the expansion of marketing.

Economic adaptation to world market conditions also has political consequences. On the one hand, it cannot be favourable to the Soviet Union to provoke conflicts with its capitalist trade partners or to be drawn into revolutionary conflicts. The successes of European détente can only favour economic co-operation. On the other hand, the capitalist states will know how to link up their political interests with their economic trade relations. The risk of political dependency cannot be ruled out.

If our assumption that the Soviet Union is dependent upon the import of capitalist technology is correct, and if it is also true that the increase of productive forces and the development of production will lead to the constant reappearance of stagnation, owing to the lack of a social dynamic, then "opening up to the world market" involves not only an expansion of foreign trade but also an increasing tie to the conditions of capitalist world market production.

If it is also true that the Soviet Union's isolation from capitalist international politics and from the capitalist world market is always a relative one, then any analysis of Soviet society must take this international area into account from the beginning. But from this point of view, problems such as those of social division and the power status of different groups of the bureaucracy are of secondary importance in evaluating Soviet society. Furthermore, all analytical approaches which investigate the conditions of production, the political system and the bureaucracy's power to govern only on the basis of internal social relations, would have to be changed. The consolidation of the socialist revolution in the form of the state and the necessary governmental organisation of socialist society, the need for the state to be a general representative abroad (and the consequences of this for the state at home), the relationship with the capitalist world market and adaptation to the preconditions dictated by this world market: all these circumstances are the basic constituents of an exact analytical definition of Soviet society.[46]

NOTES

1. For an assessment of the Soviet Union before the Second World War see Anton Pannekoek and Herman Gorter, *Organisation und Taktik der proletarischen Revolution*, edited and with an introduction by Hans Manfred Bock (Frankfurt/M. 1969); Arthur Rosenberg, *A History of Bolshevism from Marx to the First Five-Year Plan* (New York 1965); Leon Trotsky, *The Revolution*

Betrayed (New York 1957). At the present time Bettelheim and Dutschke sum up, in modified form and from different positions, the left communist critique of the Soviet Union: Charles Bettelheim, *Economic Calculations and Forms of Property* (New York 1975); Rudi Dutschke, *Versuch, Lenin auf die Füße zu stellen* (Berlin 1974). Cf. also Paul Mattick, *Marx and Keynes: the Limits of the Mixed Economy* (Boston 1969). For the trotskyist approach, cf. Ernest Mandel, "Ten Thesis on the Social and Economic Laws Governing the Society Transitional Between Capitalism and Socialism", in *Critique* 3 (1974).

2. For a summary, cf. Hansgeorg Conert, "Gibt es einen jugoslawischen Sozialismus?", in *Das Argument* 82(1973), p. 735 ff. Jahn picks up the "statism" thesis in altered form: Egbert Jahn, *Kommunismus — und was dann?* (Reinbek 1964).

3. Hillel Ticktin, "Towards a Political Economy of the USSR", in *Critique* 1 (1973), p. 20 ff; "The Relation Between the Economic Reforms and the Soviet Détente", (in this volume, p. 41). Antonio Carlo, "The Socio-Economic Nature of the USSR", in *Telos* 21 (1974); "The Structural Causes of the Soviet Policy of Coexistence" (in this volume, p. 57).

4. Ticktin, "Towards a Political Economy . . .", p. 22.

5. Ticktin, "The Relation Between . . .", p. 44 ff.; "Towards a Political Economy . . .", p. 24 ff.

6. Ticktin, "The Relation Between . . .", p. 44-5.

7. Ticktin, "Towards a Political Economy . . .", p. 36.

8. Ticktin, "Towards a Political Economy . . .", p. 27 ff.

9. It has been quite often thus described, e.g. Carlo, "The Socio-Economic Nature . . .", p. 58 ff.

10. Cf. Ticktin, "Towards a Political Economy . . .", p. 23; "The Relation Between . . .", p. 44 ff.

11. Cf. Ticktin, "Towards a Political Economy . . .", p. 23 ff.

12. Ibid., p. 34.

13. Cf. Ticktin, "The Relation Between . . .", p. 44.

14. Cf. note 4.

15. Ticktin, "Towards a Political Economy . . .", p. 38.

16. Carlo, "The Socio-Economic Nature . . .", p. 44 ff.

17. Ibid., p. 7.

18. Ibid., p. 7.

19. We by no means take it for granted that a historically higher development of human society cannot be accompanied for a period of time by an absolute or relative decline in its technical level of production. In this sense, we cannot simply designate the

People's Republic of China as "backward" in comparison with the USA.

20. Cf. section 4.

21. Carlo, "The Socio-Economic Nature . . .", p. 8.

22. The fact that at the present time the law of value has again come into favour among East Europeon economists need not indicate a subsequent recognition of objective relations. Rather, given the "marxist-leninist" level of such theorising, it is quite conceivable that it is a specific form of the inability to conceptualise — and thus to verbalise — one's own reality: a thesis which is hardly contradicted by its dehistoricising way of dealing with the marxist category of value.

23. Mandel, "Ten Theses . . .", p. 13.

24. Ibid., p. 13.

25. From this point of view, we may ask if the Russian revolution should not be reinterpreted as the classical type of revolution that occurs under conditions of "underdeveloped" structures (cf. Russia's relation to the capitalist countries of Western Europe before 1917). Since capital produces such structures (which are nonetheless not "naturally" capitalist), a revolution can only be carried out against capital — from which we can deduce the socialist claim of the Russian revolution, like that of the revolutionary movements of the third world. On the other hand, the objective character of such revolutions cannot be viewed independently of their structural preconditions. The socialist claim is denied by the concrete conditions of "underdevelopment".

26. Cf. Mandel, *Marxist Economic Theory* (New York 1969), p. 31.

27. Certainly one cannot ignore both problems; but they are to be seen as an expression of productive relations, not as the latter themselves.

28. To interpret money not as an indicator of commodity production but as a simple accounting unit (as do the Soviet economists, as well as Carlo), seems untenable to us. What purpose does such a "unit" serve? What does it express other than value, and why, if it is only an accounting aid, doesn't one simply eliminate it and replace it with letters, for example?

29. One should investigate the economic reforms of the 1950s and 60s in this context. Can they be interpreted as an attempt to let the category of value take effect in a "natural" form instead of a bureaucratic one as previously, with consumer goods prices changing according to fluctuations in production, in order to

eliminate the frictions due to the bureaucracy? From this point of view, the reforms would be a step neither in the direction of capitalism nor in that of socialism, but the putting into effect of an essentially unchanged process. The latter would then have to be investigated, as well as — at a later stage — the concrete historical circumstances of the attempt at reform.

30. The fundamental, obvious question here is, what exactly does "alienation" mean under non-capitalist conditions? An answer has not so far been given in the literature, nor can we offer one here. If we speak of "alienation" in the following pages, the concept should only be understood in its negative definition, as the social powerlessness of the producers.

31. We do not take up the significance of the Russian peasantry separately in this connection, since for quite different reasons the peasantry, no less than the industrial working population, has failed to achieve collective mastery over its own productive relations.

32. Here we can also find the general causes of defective planning and so-called purges. It is evident that the central planning authority's inability to produce a plan which functions and is safe from "sabotage" does not stem from failures on the part of the planners, but rather from the social relation between workers and state, and is thus unavoidable as long as this relation exists. In this sense, even "purges" can be seen as having their objective logic. On the one hand, the bureaucracy can only put into practice what it believes to be socialistic by means of some form of governmental compulsion; on the other hand, this brings into existence a second "apparatus" for circumventing the governmental apparatus, an apparatus of profiteers, speculators, and careerists. This apparatus can only be restrained "from above" (i.e. by means of a "purge") to the extent that it does not decisively impair the desired development, however little its socialist content might be.

33. In this contribution we cannot go into greater detail about the internal contradictions which strive for resolution. We only make the point in order to avoid giving the impression that we view the modes of functioning as impregnable, and thus as free of conflict in themselves.

34. Carlo, "The Structural Causes . . .", p. 57; Ticktin, "The Relation Between . . .", p. 7f.

35. Carlo, ibid., p. 58.

36. Ibid., p. 83 and 85 ff.

37. Ticktin, "The Relation between . . .", p. 11.
38. Ibid., p. 45.
39. Hermann Clement, "Roh- und Grundstoffe im sowjetischen Außenhandel", in Werner Gumpel and Dietmar Keese (eds.), *Probleme des Industrialismus in Ost und West: Festschrift für Hans Raupach* (Munich and Vienna, 1973).
40. Cf. also Carlo, "The Socio-Economic Nature . . .", p. 28, 31 ff. Without casting much light on the subject, Carlo insists that until 1965, regardless of trade, "the categories of the capitalist system" had no validity in the Soviet Union, while they appeared strongly afterwards. In his argument here, Carlo comes close to a "capsizing" [*Umkipp*] thesis of a type that has been posited over and over again at different times and on different occasions for the development of the Soviet Union.
41. Gripenburg, Rüdiger, "Exkurs: Zum Verhältnis von Innen- und Außenpolitik", in Wolfgang Abendroth and Kurt Lenk (eds.), *Einführung in die politische Wissenschaft* (Berne 1968), p. 167.
42. Cf. Friedrich Engels, "Die auswärtige Politik des russischen Zarentums", in Karl Marx and Friedrich Engels, *Werke* vol. XXII (Berlin 1964), p. 20. For the eighteenth century, Engels speaks of a "stateless" [*vaterlandslos*] noble bourgeois international of the enlightenment".
43. This aspect hardly enters into the discussion about the problem of the state in socialism. It is evident that the discussion itself remains attached to the separation (created by the bourgeois national state) between internal and external. Furthermore a "conservative" trait in the analysis is revealed: socialist society is conceived in a state form, as a self-enclosed, autonomous, sovereign unit which behaves as a monad in relation to other autonomous units. This discussion thus remains deficient and frequently also false.
44. Cf. also Carlo, "The Structural Causes . . .", p. 60.
45. Ticktin, "The Relation Between . . ." p. 48 ff and 50 ff; Carlo, "The Structural Causes . . .", p. 60.
46. Of course, one would then have to concretise historically the problems of the "socialist" state, of its foreign policy and its relations with the world market, and to explain them in connection with the nature of the October revolution.

6

The Soviet Union's internal problems and the development of the Warsaw Treaty Organisation

JUTTA & STEPHAN TIEDTKE

Introduction

We can explain the armaments policies of the member states of the Warsaw Treaty Organisation (WTO) by means of the action-reaction movement of the global arms race; about that there is no disagreement either in the East or in the West. From an East European point of view, this means that their own defence efforts are a result of the ever-present external threat from the capitalist countries, which is a threat to the socialist social order rather than to the territorial status quo, and that their goal is to keep up with any lead on the part of their opponents, or more generally to prevent such a lead from opening up in the first place.

In describing and explaining its armaments policies, East European literature limits itself to this model. From this literature we learn nothing of the decision-making processes which have led to this or that military policy, although there has been no lack of alternatives, even when they were reacting to the moves of an adversary. Western literature on the subject endeavours to grasp the decision-making processes partly by means of a meticulous attention to detail, but frequently by way of mere speculation. One attempts to separate the interests of the party from those of the military, or searches for conflicts of interest between representatives of different weapon systems. However carefully written these contributions may have been, so far they have not furthered discussion about the social basis of Eastern European armaments. In our contribution we have not attempted, on the basis of a still quite premature discussion about the social structure of the Eastern European states, to work out the specific character of Eastern European military policy; we have limited ourselves to investigating the extent to which (a) factors of the international system and (b) the economic interests of the Soviet Union have influenced the military policy of the WTO as a whole, and the Soviet Union in particular, within a given period of time. Moreover, we have not considered the international division of labour within the Eastern European community of states, and we have not taken up the question as to which national conflicts of interest have played a role in changes in military co-operation. Our contribution merely seeks to prove that the military posture of the Soviet Union and of the other Eastern European states is not always a simple reflex to changes within the capitalist environment, but is also marked by the internal problems of the Warsaw Treaty countries.

The period which we thought favourable for such an analysis and with which we deal in the following pages covers the years 1959 to 1961. The period seemed appropriate because during this time important decisions in Soviet military policy were reached which themselves initiated a relatively public internal discussion in the USSR. Our opening section depicts the transformation of the WTO from an actually inoperative military federation into a functioning alliance, a transformation of some importance for the East European community of states. We then investigate the influence of international tensions and the arms race (including the development of military strategy) upon the military policy of the WTO and especially the Soviet Union. The next section concerns itself with the most important decision in Soviet military policy at this time, the substantial reduction of conventional Soviet forces announced by Khrushchev at the beginning of 1960. We consider this decision, which cannot be divorced from the upgrading of the WTO, in terms of its significance for the Soviet economy.

The turning-point in the development of the Warsaw Treaty Organisation at the beginning of the 1960s

In the Western literature on the subject, there is a current notion that in the period from 1955 to 1960-61, which was the first phase of the Warsaw Treaty's development, political rather than military questions stood in the foreground of the organisation's activities. In an intersystemic context, this is explained as a diplomatic measure for preventing West Germany from enlisting in NATO, or equally as an attempt to dismantle NATO by means of a proposed reciprocal dismantling of the WTO. If, on the other hand, one seeks the causes in the East European system, the explanation is that the military integration of Eastern Europe was certainly planned from the beginning, but was postponed because of the events in Poland and Hungary in 1956.

The infrequent meetings of the WTO's highest body, the Political Consultative Committee (PCC), points in particular to the provisional nature of the WTO's military tasks;[1] from February 1956 to 1960 the PCC met a total of only three times instead of at least twice yearly, as prescribed by the Warsaw Treaty statutes, and political questions stood in the foreground of these meetings. At this time, the purely military apparatus of the WTO, with its joint command at the top, was only a "paper organisation".[2]

The state of military co-operation in the WTO during its first phase can be summarised as follows:[3]

> "In the first phase, lasting about five years after the formation of the Warsaw Pact in May 1955, the military contributions of the East European armed forces apparently carried little more weight in Soviet planning than had been the case in Stalin's day. Apart from the improvement of joint air defence arrangements in Eastern Europe, the Soviet Union made no major effort to weld the Warsaw Pact into an integrated military alliance."[4]

Along with the improvement of the WTO's joint air defence system, which was under the direct control of the air defence system of the Soviet Union, there were additional advances in military co-operation during this initial phase of the WTO which simultaneously affected all Warsaw Treaty states: in the standardisation of weapons, in the adoption of Soviet forms of military organisation and doctrine, and in the definition of military tasks for individual East European armed forces. As a sign of military co-ordination, we may also take cognizance of the fact that the Warsaw Treaty states carried out parallel manpower reductions. From 1955 to 1957 the Soviet armed forces (1955: 5.763 million men) were reduced by 1.84 million men,[5] and the remaining Warsaw Treaty armies by 402,500 men).[6] These troop reductions were approved by the PCC (although subsequently) at its second meeting in May 1958. As a whole, the Western literature has interpreted this stage of military co-operation as one that merely enabled the Warsaw Treaty armed forces to embark upon an ensuing phase of military co-operation, of which, however, there were no signs before 1960.[7]

The East European literature, whose divisions into phases correspond by and large to those in the Western literature, argues differently. In retrospect, it presents the first phase as a purposeful stage of construction for the second phase, the period of greater military co-operation. The literature of the German Democratic Republic, for example, states:

> "The period from 1956 to 1961 was one in which the bases for the formation of the National People's Army as a modern socialist army were improved and made solid. . . .[8]
>
> The founding period of the socialist military coalition was followed by a time of consolidation, which essentially covered the years 1956-1960."[9]

In the second phase of Warsaw Treaty development, which commenced in 1960-61 and lasted until 1964-65 (i.e. the change of administration in the Soviet Union), the organisation — if one follows the Western literature — took shape as a functioning military alliance.[10] In this period the political activity of the organisation was very low in comparison with the military activity.[11] Kosygin's speech to the Supreme Soviet in December 1964 first re-emphasised the political aspects of the organisation.[12] Thomas Wolfe views the situation after 1960 as follows:

> "Over the next few years, the new policy line had the general effect of upgrading the Warsaw Pact publicly in terms of the common defence of the communist camp. More specifically, it served to elevate the importance of the military contribution of non-Soviet Pact countries in overall Soviet planning; to extend the mission of the East European forces from primary emphasis on air defence to a more active role in defensive and offensive theatre operations . . ."[13]

In contrast to the 1950s, in which only the joint air defence systems of the WTO were preferentially equipped with modern weapons, at the beginning of the 1960s the Soviet government proceeded to equip non-Soviet Treaty armies to a greater extent with modern weapons:[14] the medium T-34 tank was replaced to a large extent by the T-54, which had been in operation in the Soviet army since 1954; and the East European armed forces received advanced combat aircraft such as the MIG-21 interceptor plane and the SU7 fighter bomber, which had both been used in the Soviet armed forces since 1959.[15] The equipment of non-Soviet Warsaw Treaty armies with tactical missiles, exhibited for the first time in summer 1964 at military parades in Eastern Europe, also belongs to this programme of upgrading.[16] One possibility for expressing the modernised equipment of the WTO armed forces in absolute figures is the amount of PS that the average soldier has had at his disposal. The following figures exist for the NPA:[17]

1958	25.4 PS*	per soldier
1964	29.1 PS	per soldier
1971	30.5 PS	per soldier

Along with this technological data,[18] a series of additional factors pointed to a change in the military and political significance of the Warsaw Treaty Organisation:

(1) In July 1960, A. A. Grechko became Commander-in-chief of the Warsaw Pact joint armed forces. Grechko was previously Commander (in-chief) of the Group of Soviet Forces in East Germany (until 1957), and later Commander of Soviet Ground Forces (1957 to 1960).[19]

(2) An increase in the meetings of the PCC: February 1960; March 1961; June 1962.

(3) In September 1961 the first known conference of defence ministers of the Warsaw Treaty states took place, followed by conferences in January 1962 and February 1963.

(4) The new party programme of the Communist Party of the Soviet Union, announced in July 1961, demanded increased integration of the WTO.

---

* The German term *Pferde Stärke* (PS) is similar, but not equivalent, to the English term "horsepower".

(5) In October-November, 1961, the first joint manoeuvres of
   several WTO states took place. Since that time, numerous
   joint manoeuvres have taken place each year.

The East German literature establishes the beginning of a
"qualitatively higher stage", both in the development of the NPA
and in that of the WTO, for the years following 1960:

> "At the beginning of the 1960s, there commenced a new
> development of the NPA which lasted until 1965. . . .
> Socialist home defence was built up as a whole and the
> potential of the social order sufficed for an effective increase
> of defence capability. That enabled the NPA to fulfil new
> demands which corresponded to a growing contribution to
> the collective protection of socialism. The military solidarity
> and the co-operation of the NPA and of the Soviet army and
> of other armed forces of the coalition attained a qualitatively
> higher stage."[20]

The "qualitatively higher stage" in ordnance and co-operation
reached its completion about 1962:

> "In the training year 1962, it was therefore possible to
> pass over to a higher stage of military co-operation of the
> NPA with its allied forces . . ."[21]
> "Supported by the overall help of the Soviet Union and by
> further improvements in the economic co-operation of the
> GDR with all the states of the socialist community, the NPA
> was able to rapidly renovate its ordnance and equip-
> ment . . ."[22]

If one accepts these statements and the presentation of the first
phase of the WTO in the military literature of the GDR, the turning-point after 1960 is primarily a military event internal to the
pact, a necessary result of "scientific, technical progress and the
revolution in the armed forces"[23] and of long-range planning, and
obviously little influenced by international events. This interpretation does not, of course, exclude the possibility of legitimising
the increased defence efforts of the socialist states as a whole by
reason of "intensified class antagonism between socialism and
capitalism."[24]

*Foreign policy reasons for the military upgrading of the Warsaw
Treaty Organisation*

Changes in the international system, influencing the Soviet Union's
decision to transfer larger military burdens to its partners in the
Warsaw Treaty Organisation, were to be expected in the context
of the tensions surrounding Berlin after 1958 and in the development of the arms race. We could easily detect the influence, if
only it were possible to determine the point at which the decision
to restructure the WTO was reached. But we run into difficulties
here. The East German literature quoted earlier sometimes ends
the first phase of Warsaw Treaty development in 1960 and at
other times in 1961, or refers to a transitional phase which ended
in 1962. The other available indicators of the WTO arms build-up
point equally well to 1960 or to 1961. Western dating vacillates
accordingly, but for the most part Western observers content
themselves with identifying what was most salient to them — the
massive arms build-up starting from Summer 1961 — with the
beginning of the changes.[25] The American specialist for East European military problems, Thomas W. Wolfe, involuntarily discovered how changeable and uncertain datings in this context can
be, when he asserted that there were already changes in the Soviet
interpretation of the role of non-Soviet Treaty forces at the end
of the 1950s,[26] but could only find unmistakable signs of this
change after 1960-61, as a result of the worsening situation in
Europe and the open outbreak of the Sino-Soviet conflict.[27]

The international tensions at the beginning of the 1960s, which
reached their high point in the Berlin crisis (August 1961) and
the Cuban missile crisis (October 1962), at first glance provide an
explanation for the Soviet decision to upgrade the WTO. But the
fact that the WTO did not participate in the Berlin crisis as a
military organisation (which was not the case in the Cuban crisis,
when the WTO forces were put on alert) contradicts the idea of
an immediate relation between the Berlin crisis and the upgrading
of the WTO.[28] Formally speaking, neither the Berlin crisis (because
it was a four-power question) nor the Cuban missile conflict
(because it lay outside the territorial limits of the WTO) fell
within the organisation's competence. Apart from the PCC meeting of March 1961, which dealt with the problem of German

policy and of WTO co-operation, the improvement in military co-operation first became visible after the crisis had subsided.[29] We may cite as evidence the first meeting of defence ministers in September 1961 and the first common manoeuvres of the Warsaw Treaty Organisation in October-November 1961.

The one major and demonstrative military measure in Eastern Europe which can be placed in the immediate context of the Berlin crisis — in which the WTO was not directly involved — was the decision of the Soviet government on 8 July 1961 to suspend the troop reduction programme which had been announced on 14 January 1960, and to raise the defence budget from 9.3 to 12.4 billion rubles instead of reducing it to 9.26 billion rubles, as had been anticipated. But this Soviet decision seems rather to have been a reaction to the preceding large-scale American arms decisions than to have been influenced by the Berlin crisis. In contrast to simultaneous American decisions announced in March 1961 by Kennedy — an increase in the defence budget of 3.5 billion dollars, substantial increases in military manpower and improvement of the ordnance of American ground forces, and the construction of 800 ICBMs and 40 Polaris submarines[30] — the Soviets let it be known that their decision was only a temporary one, which would be withdrawn given a corresponding improvement in the international climate. In December 1963, after the tensions had eased, Khrushchev actually held out the prospect of new military manpower reductions and a decrease in the military budget.[32] If the Soviet defence measures had been related to the Berlin crisis, they could have been expected at a much earlier date, and at least after the U-2 incident in May 1960, which has been interpreted as resulting from the Soviet assessment that the USA could not be moved to a compromise on the Berlin question.[33] But if one accepts Khrushchev's assertions at the time, the incident had no influence upon the military policy pursued after the beginning of 1960.[34]

One can thus conclude with some certainty that the acute tension in international relations as a result of the Berlin crisis did not immediately initiate the WTO's arms build-up. Nevertheless, one can detect a connection between the Warsaw Pact arms build-up and the tensions in Berlin in the summer of 1961. One should not, however, interpret the connection to imply that the crisis inaugurated intensive military co-operation. Rather, one must ask whether the economic and military integration undertaken by the East European states did not necessitate this Berlin crisis and its solution (the erection of the "wall"): that is to say, whether the economic and social consolidation of East Germany — an essential presupposition of East European integration — did not depend to a large degree upon secluding East Germany from the West. But seclusion must be understood in the sense of military integration too, since it was thereby possible to cut off the flow of military information carried to the West by refugee military personnel.

In what international context does the East European literature present the arms build-up of the WTO or, to use its own terminology, the "effective increase of defence capability"?[35] In answering this question, we face difficulties with the Soviet literature, because simultaneously with the arms build-up of the WTO, the Soviet Union undertook disarmament measures (the troop reductions of 1960 were propagated as such)which cannot be reconciled with the tense international situation, since this latter should have strengthened the security considerations of the military against troop reductions. A Soviet pamphlet which dates from 1960 sets out the need to improve internal pact co-operation in the following international context:

> "Under the present-day international situation, the countries of the socialist world system must still expand their economic co-operation, their political unity, by uniting their military efforts in order to co-ordinate their defence measures."[36]

Against the background of Western defence measures — the USA's 1959 decision to increase defence expenditures, and its ten-year plan for NATO — Bashkardin poses the need for the socialist countries not to act independently of one another in the face of this development.[37] But Khrushchev assessed the international situation quite differently in his speech of 14 January 1960, in which he announced the reduction of conventional troops by 1.2 million: "We have repeatedly emphasised already that the international situation has decisively improved in recent times".[38] This contradiction might suggest a certain difficulty in the justification of Soviet military and WTO policy at the beginning of

the 1960s. But from an East European point of view the relation
between détente and arms policy is self-evident. Looking back to
the period around 1960:

> "With a new quality in the growth of the socialist world
> system at the beginning of the 1960s, there also began a
> new stage in the improvement and consolidation of the
> socialist military coalition. Taking into account the changed
> balance of power in the world in favour of socialism, it
> was deemed possible — at the meeting of representatives
> of communist and workers' parties in 1960 in Moscow — to
> compel the NATO countries to peaceful coexistence, relying
> on the military strength of the Warsaw Treaty, in particular
> on the missile and atomic forces of the Soviet Union. At the
> same time, the necessity was emphasised of constantly build-
> ing up the defence capability of the socialist community."[39]

In order to explain the development of intensive military co-
operation within the WTO as a result of the arms race, one must
show that in the period around 1960 the balance of power
between NATO and the WTO had changed or threatened to
change so much that an arms build-up of the WTO had become
necessary, involving changes in strategy too, since these usually
depend upon the further development of weapons systems.

Let us first consider the arms race. From an East European
point of view, the arms race presented itself at the end of the
1960s or the beginning of the 1960s quite simply: reports from
Eastern Europe at the time uniformly asserted a military
superiority of the socialist camp over NATO in all essential
defence sectors.[40] In particular, the Soviet Union insisted again
and again in official declarations upon its superiority in strategic
weapons:

> "We are several years in advance of other countries in the
> development and mass production of intercontinental
> ballistic missiles of various types."[41]

This ostensibly advanced development of Soviet missile potential was underlined by the establishment of strategic missiles as
the fifth branch of the Soviet armed forces in May 1960. Other
areas in which superiority over the West was claimed, but which

were not so widely publicised, were (a) disposal of a greater human potential, which was in addition supposed to be morally superior; (b) planned reserve readiness in case of mobilisation; (c) the ability to adapt the economy rapidly to war needs; (d) a good transport system; (e) a favourable territorial division of industry.[42] If one takes the Soviet claim to superiority at face value, one can dispense with further research, and American pressure in the arms race would be responsible for the WTO re-armament. Given the source materials, it is futile to ask why the Soviet Union laid claim to such superiority in the first place and in such a demonstrative fashion (especially in strategic weapons); first of all this superiority did not exist, although this was recog-nised in the USA only in 1960,[43] and secondly such stereotyped repetitions of its claim to superiority were an explicit challenge to its opponent to break its superiority — a challenge resolutely picked up by the USA at the end of the 1950s. In this sense, we can actually speak of a stepping up of the arms race by the Soviet Union. The actual quantitative balance of power in strategic weapons of the two superpowers at the beginning of the 1960s looked approximately as follows:[44]

		1959	1960	1961	1962	1963	1964	1965
USA	ICBM*	none	18	63	294	424	834	1054
USSR	ICBM	some	35	50	75	100	200	1050
USA	SLBM**	none	32	96	144	224	416	656
USSR	SLBM	none	none	some	some	100	120	160

We could adduce the following points as possible reasons for the Soviet claim to superiority. The first is that strategic superiority was claimed in order to calm domestic Soviet anxieties about security, occasioned by the quantitatively significant reduc-tion of conventional troops after 1960.[45] There is evidence for such a connection with troop reductions in the fact that Khrush-chev expressed his most extreme Soviet claim to superiority in January 1960.[46] The second argument could be that there was an attempt to exert pressure upon disarmament negotiations; at this time, the Soviet Union was taking the initiative in disarma-

---

* Land-based intercontinental ballistic missiles.
** Submarine-launched ballistic missiles.

ment negotiations.[47] And the third argument could be that the strategic superiority, which was taken at face value in the West because of the USSR's spectacular successes in space research, was to have a deterrent function against possible attack from the United States and give the Soviet Union military security during this transitional period. (This argument is related to the one which claims that the Soviet Union has only claimed superiority during periods of actual military inferiority.)

The question of armaments reorganisation occupied an essential place in discussions of Soviet military policy just before the 1960s, especially when there was a need to explain the Soviet troop reductions of 1960. Under the assumption that such a reorganisation actually took place, one can posit the thesis that the Soviet Union transferred greater military burdens to its WTO partners in order not to have to greatly increase its own defence budget with the additional construction of strategic weapons. The supposed financial pressures on the Soviet defence budget, resulting from an expansion of the strategic missile programme, have been generally accepted by Western commentators.[48] In his January 1960 speech, Khrushchev encouraged such belief when he asserted, among other things, that:

> "The weapons which we now have are awe-inspiring, but those which are in the offing, as it were, will be even more awe-inspiring and refined. The weapons which have been developed and are, so to speak, locked up in the vaults of the scientists and engineers, these are incredibly powerful weapons."[49]

According to Bloomfield, the programme for Soviet missile development at the beginning of the 1960s included the development and mass production of second-generation ICBMs and the further development of submarine capacity,[50] and not the construction of first-generation missiles (as was believed in the West by those who supported an overestimate of Soviet missile potential — a false assumption that was subsequently promoted by the Soviet Union).[51]

If we are to speak about reorganisation at all, a necessary condition is that along with cutbacks in military manpower, some weapons systems are dismantled. But Khrushchev also made the following announcement in his speech:

> "Missiles have almost completely replaced our air forces.
> We have now strongly limited our air forces and will prob-
> ably undertake an additional decrease in or even halt the
> production of bombers and other outdated technical means.
> In the navy, the submarine fleet has taken on an enormous
> significance, but conventional ships can no longer play the
> role which they played in the past."[52]

In the case of the Soviet air force, the dismantling of material
appeared to be more or less as follows. The effective number of
aeroplanes was reduced from 20,000 in 1959 to 12,500 in 1963,[53]
the majority of the aeroplanes being put out of service at the
beginning of the 1960s.[54] Khrushchev's assertions notwithstanding,
long-range bombers remained untouched by this development.
One can in fact detect an increase in this area after 1960:[55]

	1960	1961	1965
USA	450	600	630
USSR	150	190	200

Did these reductions in manpower level and in weapons systems
actually become necessary because of the increased costs of
developing and producing ICBMs? Several different factors con-
tradict such a direct connection. First of all, the long-range planning required for modern weapons systems means that one would
not expect an immediate increase in costs for strategic weapons.[56]
Secondly, the Soviet Union did not excessively push the development of its ICBM capacities at the beginning of the 1960s. During
the Khrushchev era, the USSR made no effort to achieve strategic
parity with the USA.[57] Thirdly, Soviet ICBMs went into mass
production significantly later and not, as Khrushchev asserted,
as early as 1959. And finally, a direct redistribution of freed
resources, previously used for conventional troops, is only possible to a limited extent in developing and producing strategic
weapons systems:

> "Modern strategic systems were thus more in direct com-
> petition with the advanced technology and skills needed for
> expanding new growth sectors of the economy than with the
> resources of traditional industry, which supported the theatre

forces. To meet the build-up of strategic forces, Khrushchev could therefore not expect to free resources directly simply by cutting back theatre forces." [58]

In his speech of January 1960, Khrushchev did not reject the reorganisation theory, which was already current during the preceding troop reduction, but vehemently attacked Western suggestions that savings created by the troop cutbacks were to be used to get the Soviet Union out of an economic blind alley.[59] V. A. Sorin certainly refutes Western supporters of the reorganisation thesis, by referring to the fact that the resources freed by the troop reduction were legitimately tied to non-military purposes.[60] Nevertheless, the Soviet literature also encourages the belief that a reorganisation had taken place during this period — although the term "reorganisation" [*perevooruzhenie*] crops up only rarely,[61] and then usually refers to a long-range adaptation of the armed forces to the changed conditions of the nuclear age. Alternatively, this impression results from the Soviet claim to superiority in strategic weapons:

> "Fundamental changes in the area of equipment, combat technique, structure, theory, warfare, practice and the education and training of troops, were effectively concluded by the end of 1961. In the military a new revolution had taken place: the Soviet armed forces had qualitatively changed, the combat capability and readiness had grown immeasurably."[62]

Although the Soviet account of the balance of power in strategic weapons between the two superpowers in no way corresponds to reality, during this time the Soviet leadership did not hesitate to make atomic weapons virtually the sole determining factor in its *strategy*. This suggests that the Soviet Union was at this time pursuing a concept of "minimum deterrent", according to which they could successfully deter their opponents if only some nuclear missiles were certain to reach their target. Khrushchev's remarks in May 1960 permit one, perhaps, to make such an interpretation: "missiles are not cucumbers, one cannot eat them and one does not require more than a certain number in order to ward off an attack".[63] The officially proclaimed Soviet military strategy, which had unlimited validity at the time of the troop reduction programme, assumed that a future world war which was no longer viewed as unavoidable,[64] or likewise a war in Europe, would quickly escalate into nuclear strategic dimensions and be decided by nuclear weapons. In terms of this strategy, conventional forces retained only negligible tasks — for example, occupying the opponent's territory after the decisive nuclear exchange. Only on the basis of this strategy, which shifted the militarily decisive contribution of conventional forces into the background, could the troop cutbacks of 1960 be justified from the point of view of security. But how is one to explain this nuclear strategy in view of the fact that the Soviet WTO partners upgraded their conventional forces after 1960, and thus at a moment when the Soviet Union was substantially reducing its conventional forces? The question is all the more vital inasmuch as the Soviet Union and its WTO partners reduced their conventional forces in the second half of the 1950s according to the same strategic principle.[65]

In explaining this contradiction in Soviet military policy, we must consider two possibilities. The first explanation is that the military upgrading of conventional WTO forces was the first response of the East European military apparatus to changes in American strategy during the 1950s. At the end of the Eisenhower era, even if the concept of "massive retaliation" had not been replaced by that of "graduated deterrence", it had at least been questioned. The final retreat from the strategy of massive retaliation first occurred during the Kennedy administration, with Kennedy's official presentation of the doctrine of "flexible response" in his special message of 8 March 1961 and the corresponding American defence measures. The concept of "graduated deterrence" already included the demand for an increase of conventional forces in the West European NATO countries.

The second possibility is that the Soviet military, in particular the representatives of conventional forces, could only be moved to agree to the programme of troop reduction when Khrushchev offered an arms build-up of the allied armed forces in the WTO as compensation for conventional disarmament in the Soviet Union. This thesis is approximately that of Kolkowicz and Wolfe. Kolkowicz asserts that the non-Soviet WTO armed forces were to "fill the gap which had arisen through the reduction of conventional forces."[67] Wolfe sees the strengthening of WTO capability as a "rationale for the decrease in one's own ground forces, the rationale that a larger portion of the military costs and burden could be borne by the East European allies."[68]

During the Khrushchev era there were no tendencies in Soviet strategy which could be compared with the American strategy of "flexible response": only at the end of the Khrushchev period could one discover signs of thinking along these lines in the Soviet military debate.[69] The transfer of military burdens thus did not mean a transfer of decisive military tasks to the WTO partners, as long as Soviet strategy attached little importance to conventional forces. What took place was merely a rough military balancing out of non-Soviet and Soviet conventional forces. The imbalance consisted, among other things, in the fact that the WTO armed forces were equipped with tactical nuclear weapons later than were the Soviet armed forces — probably only from 1964 on — and that the warheads of these nuclear weapons always remained under Soviet lock and key.

A military-strategic upgrading of the conventional forces of the Soviet Union and its WTO partners took place, then, after the middle of 1961, supposedly as a result of American arms decisions in March 1961. But this upgrading occurred within the framework of the still nominally maintained strategy of massive retaliation, as one can see from Malinovski's speech to the twenty-second congress of the Communist Party of the Soviet Union in October 1961:

> "Apart from the fact that in a future war missiles — and nuclear weapons — would occupy the most important position, we have arrived at the conclusion that ultimate victory over the aggressor could only be attained by means of the common action of all branches of the armed forces. For that reason, we give the necessary attention to the refinement of all weapons systems, and teach the armed forces to master them and to achieve the decisive victory over the aggressor. Moreover, we are of the belief that under present conditions a future world war, in spite of enormous losses, will be waged with armed forces numbering into millions."[70]

The consequence of this change for the WTO can be observed,

for example, in the different attitudes towards military service in East Germany between 1960 and 1962. The declaration of the fourth PCC meeting on 4 February 1960, which approved the Soviet decision to reduce conventional forces, still hailed the "positive example of East Germany" in having voluntarily renounced any introduction of the draft.[71] But on 24 January 1962, East Germany nevertheless resolved upon a system of universal conscription which would enable the National People's Army "to systematically expand its personnel from the ranks of young workers" and to "undertake responsibility for strengthening the collective defence force of socialism to a necessary degree."[72]

In short it can be stated that the arms race had only secondary importance, if indeed it had any at all, for the military upgrading of the WTO. The increased military contribution of the WTO armed forces did not have the function of strengthening the combat capability of the Warsaw Treaty as a whole, but took the place of the reduced Soviet potential. This redistribution programme also includes the possibility that the Soviet WTO partners indirectly contributed to the reorganisation costs of the Soviet armed forces by meeting part of what had previously been the USSR's expenses for the conventional equipment of its armed forces. If this corresponds to historical reality, the question which underlies our next section still remains. Why did the Soviet Union at the beginning of the 1960s turn away from its previously practised concept of almost exclusively bearing the economic burden of defence for the socialist camp? Since a change in Soviet military strategy did not take place in 1960, we must exclude the possibility that changes of strategy were a motive for upgrading the WTO. At the same time, it was the very fact that there was no retreat from the Soviet strategy of massive retaliation that constituted the strategic prerequisite for the Soviet military reductions of 1960. From the middle of 1961, as the Soviet Union's conventional forces took on a new importance in strategy, but without a change of strategy, the newly undertaken military upgrading of the WTO was decisively shifted in the direction of greater joint military responsibility.

*The economic background of Soviet military policy at the
beginning of the 1960s*

In analysing the internal Soviet factors which conditioned the
changes in Soviet military policy towards the WTO, we start from
the assumption that largely identical motives underlay both the
Soviet decision to upgrade the WTO and the simultaneous
military-political measures which only affected the Soviet armed
forces. This means that we presuppose an immediate connection
between the WTO arms build-up and the most important military-
political measure within the Soviet armed forces at that time, the
substantial reduction of conventional (i.e. non-strategic) Soviet
forces announced in January 1960. We believe that if we investigate the economic background of the manpower reductions in
detail, we can thereby at least partly explain the interest of the
Soviet leadership in a WTO arms build-up. This premise is tenable
for various reasons. Both military decisions affected only the conventional forces; the decision to upgrade the WTO came largely
from the Soviet Union; these events took place almost simultaneously; and as we have already stated, the international situation
cannot be considered as a determinant in the Soviet decision (it
only played a role to the extent that a relatively relaxed international situation was a precondition for such changes).

We shall now concern ourselves with the influence of economic
problems of the Soviet Union upon the military decisions at the
beginning of 1960, and more particularly with (1) the planning
of the troop cutbacks in connection with the labour situation,
especially regional shortages of labour in the Soviet Union; (2) the
planned use of financial resources freed by the troop cutbacks;
(3) other decisions in Soviet military policy, which were aimed
at keeping the economic costs of the military apparatus as low as
possible.[73]

In the years after 1955 the Soviet Union carried out troop
reductions from a 1955 manpower total of 5.763 million men:[74]

1955	640,000	discharged military personnel
1956/57	1,200,000	,, ,, ,,
1958-1960	300,000	,, ,, ,,
1960 (planned)	1,200,000	,, ,, ,,

The troop cutback to 2.423 million men announced on 14 January 1960 was to have been completed "by autumn 1961";[75] but in July 1961 it was postponed by order of the Supreme Soviet.[76] From a very early point, Western writers connected this troop cutback with the shortage of labour in the Soviet Union, but without offering a thorough analysis of this connection.[77] At the end of the 1950s, the labour situation in the Soviet Union became precarious for various reasons. The justification for carrying out the 1959 census (the first since 1939) showed an awareness of the problem:

> "One of the most important tasks of the census consists in making available initial data for determining the labour reserves of Soviet society . . . as well as determining the possibility of an incorporation of additional labour reserves . . . into social production."[78]

The shortage of labour in the Soviet Union is — as we shall see in detail — more a regional and structural one than an overall economic one, as the Soviet Union itself constantly emphasises.[79]

Nevertheless, we shall present some data about the overall economic labour situation in order to give an idea of the economic relevance of 1.2 million ex-soldiers to the economy. From 1956 to 1958 the Soviet Union added 6.2 million people to its labour force, or 2.66 million per year. According to the seven-year plan (1959 to 1965), which is of special interest in this context, approximately twelve million persons were to be recruited to the labour force, a yearly average of 1.7 million.[81] In accounting for the comparatively high hiring quotas of the years 1956 to 1958, one must remember that during this time substantial troop reductions — 1.5 million men — were carried out.[82]

The planned recruiting of twelve million additional persons to the labour force during the first seven-year plan was to be achieved in the first place by a further exhaustion of labour reserves; troop reductions were evidently not foreseen as a means of fulfilling this figure.[83] But the following digression shows on what shaky ground the seven-year plan had to proceed in this area.

The figures for the labour reserves, i.e. persons "who are occupied in their own collective economic activity, as well as young people who have reached the age of employment"[84] — members of the military are thus excluded from this group — provide information about the degree of exhaustion of the potential. These figures, calculated from the total of non-gainfully employed people of working age — men between 16 and 59 years, women between 16 and 54 years — nevertheless tell us little about the actual availability of labour.[85]

In the Soviet planned economy, available and required labour is determined or established according to a "labour force balance".[86] But the accounts of this balance are quite inaccurate; they are conditioned by deficient or incomplete statistical data, numerous formal defects and systemic peculiarities, such as the inclination of many plants to keep "silent reserves" of labour on the side. Moreover, the problem of migration, one of the basic problems of the Soviet labour market,[87] is not adequately dealt with, so that there are substantial defects in the calculations.[88] Apart from a lack of precision, the determination of the extent of labour reserves is also complicated by the fact that the results are dependent upon how the possibilities for mobilising the available reserves are estimated, and therefore differ widely. In the year 1965, for example, the calculations vary between six million and twenty million.[89]

Even the previously acknowledged reasons for a decreasing trend in the release of new labour resources were partly not confirmed by the actual development. Three reasons in particular, connected with the troop reductions, should be mentioned:

(1) The traditional labour reservoir of unemployed women began to run out.[90] However, this prognosis, often asserted by Western writers, did not hold true until 1963: while women accounted for 47% of the total number of workers and white collar employees (26.56 million) in 1959, the portion rose to 49% (34.30 million).[91] Since the percentage participation of women increased particularly in those occupations[92] and regions[93] in which discharged military personnel could not find work, as will be shown later, this influx into the labour force is of only limited relevance for our analysis.

(2) The additional drain of labour from the countryside was still possible only at the expense of agricultural capacity;[94] nevertheless, migration from the country continued. According to Soviet

data, the exodus from the land accounted for 1.3 million persons yearly from 1959 to 1965, with a special loss of males (53%) and those aged between 16 and 34 (70%).[95] At the same time, "a significant portion of qualified cadres emigrated from the land, especially mechanics" (i.e. farm machine specialists).[96] The labour problem in agriculture — the lack of specialists, the ageing agrarian population (its average age in the RSFSR is fifty) and the high proportion of women — became proportionately more acute. The plans for troop cutbacks in 1960 therefore show the reverse tendency: discharged soldiers are to be employed as specialists in agriculture. Moreover, one of the "civilian tasks" of the army consists in offering technical help to agriculture.[97]

(3) War losses and the resulting severe drop in the birth rate had caused a decrease of the natural influx of labour. The full effect of this birth lag must have made itself felt in the years 1959 to 1965, when the war generation reached the age of employment.[98] This means that in 1960, maintaining the troop strength of the Soviet armed forces must necessarily have decreased the influx of young male labourers into the production process. Just how desperate the situation was in the case of this generation became evident in 1961, when military considerations forced the suspension of the troop cutbacks. At that time, the age of compensation had to be lowered from 19 to 17 years;[99] only in this way could one compensate for the low birthrate of 1943.

With the exhaustion of the traditional labour reservoir, the Soviet Union attempted to meet the labour shortage by all possible means. The following measures, taken at the end of the 1950s, were directly or indirectly connected with the worsening labour supply situation: (1) administrative reforms in industry, construction and agriculture as well as in the planning system (1957, 1958); (2) the intensification of unpaid labour in lower administrative units, and the simultaneous reduction of full-time positions (from 1957); (3) reforms of the educational system (1958); (4) the intensification of socialist competition, with the introduction of the "movement for communist labour" (around 1959); (5) reductions in working time (from 1958). In Western literature, this last measure is usually cited as proof of a Soviet labour surplus.[100] But this argument does not hold up since, for a given level of productivity, the maintenance of an overextended working day would prevent further increases in productivity.

The Soviet economic planners saw the increase of productivity as a decisive escape from the dilemma of the labour shortage.[101] But as it turned out, two factors stood in the way of increasing productivity. First of all, the capital goods necessary for increasing productivity were highly scarce, especially in comparison with investments for other projects in the seven-year plan;[102] just to open up the "natural resources of the Eastern region . . . it would have been necessary according to the seven-year plan to direct over 40% of all investments into this region."[103] And secondly, the factories attempted to circumvent the introduction of new techniques necessary for increasing production, since the necessary investments for conversion would have threatened the fulfilment of their individual plans.[104]

The lack of labour, the difficulty of mobilising labour reserves and the low increase in labour productivity[105] are among the essential reasons why the goals of the first seven-year plan, scaled down from those of the prematurely abandoned five-year plan of 1957, could not be reached even in the initial phase.[106]

If the troop reduction was to be used as a means for over-coming these complex difficulties with the labour force, it could only be successful if it succeeded in winning over discharged military personnel for the elimination of the regional and partly structural shortage of labour. Otherwise it was all too probable that the multitude of discharged soldiers would remain unused economically, or would even augment the regional labour surplus.

Since the compulsion to remain at one's job was eliminated in 1956, a considerable internal migration has taken place, which has assumed alarming proportions for Soviet economic planning.[107] These migrations, which take place largely out of governmental control and whose causes we cannot deal with here, caused (among other things) labour from areas with a labour deficit to wander into areas with a labour surplus. In particular, the Eastern regions of the Soviet Union, whose industrialisation had already received high priority among the tasks of the Soviet economy in the sixth five-year plan (1956 to 1960, abandoned in 1957), show a negative balance of migration. This internal "colonisation of the East", which was to have been carried out exclusively by "free" labourers, itself claimed half of all capital investments.[108] The

seven-year plan retained the preferential development of the
Eastern region.[109] In spite of comprehensive socio-political
measures to stem migration[110] "which does not correspond to our
economic plans",[111] emigration from West Siberia between 1959
and 1962 exceeded the number of immigrants by a quarter of a
million.[112] The costs which arose from the fluctuation in the
labour force were enormous: "According to our preceding
calculations, the losses occurring to the economy of the USSR
owing to fluctuations of the labour force accounted for two
billion rubles annually, the largest share going to the regions of
the Urals, Siberia and the Far East".[113] In the view of Soviet
experts, the labour demand in East and West Siberia (leaving
aside the Far East) during the seven-year plan accounted for at
least 1.5 million workers and white-collar employees.[114] According
to another Soviet estimate, fulfilment of the seven-year plan
depended to a large extent upon the achievement of an increase
of the urban population in the Eastern regions of at least 5% —
which would have meant an increase in the total population in
these regions of about five million.[115]

Along with the economic considerations, there were also
military considerations involved in industrialising the East, which
were obvious if we look at the initial phase of the second world
war. In his work on the significance of the socialist camp's
economic potential in relation to its defence capability, N. A.
Bashkardin advocated the industrialisation of the East in the
following terms:

> "Such a division of productive forces in the Soviet Union
> fully corresponds to the task of strengthening the economic
> power of our country and the vital capacities of the economy
> in the case of a war."[116]

The regional division of labour in the USSR as a whole yielded
the following picture at the beginning of the 1960s:

Extent of available labour reserves	Regions of the USSR
1. Lack of labour power	Northwest; West Siberia; East Siberia; Far East; Kazakhstan
2. Sufficient quantity of labour power	Volga Region; Urals; Baltic Republics

3. Excess of labour power   Centre; North Caucasus; White Russia; Ukraine; Moldavia; Transcaucasus; Middle Asia

According to the seven-year plan, the Ukraine and the Transcaucasus were envisaged as principal suppliers of labour for the Eastern regions and Kazakhstan. "Within a very short time it became clear that these calculations were misleading";[118] economic and socio-political obstacles stood in the way of resettlement.[119] Labour planning for the Eastern regions had thus already gone aground at the beginning of the seven-year plan. For our purposes, this raises the question: were the troop cutbacks of January 1960 seized upon as a means for dealing with the seven-year plan's negative development of labour potential?

In the first part of this essay, we attempted to show that before 1960 there were no signs of a military upgrading of the WTO; there were no declarations of intent, nor was there a trend to military co-operation which would have led one to expect such a development. Obviously, the Soviet decision to carry out troop cutbacks was reached at short notice. This can be viewed as an additional pointer to the connection between the upgrading of the WTO and the troop reductions. Alexander Volkov, chairman of the State Committee for Labour and Wages in the cabinet council of the USSR, asserted at the beginning of February 1960 that the demobilisation of parts of the Soviet armed forces had never been under consideration in labour planning for the seven-year plan.[120] But Volkov's statement leaves open the possibility that the troop cutbacks were involved in labour planning at a later date. The fact that in March 1959, at a time when the seven-year plan had already been put into effect, Khrushchev was still decisively rejecting the possibility of further troop reductions, favours such a notion:

"We can and will not unilaterally withdraw our troops [from East Germany]. And I will go so far as to say that we do not intend unilaterally to make further reductions in our armed forces, since the Soviet Union has already reduced its forces by more than 2 million men."[121]

Starting therefore from the assumption that the troop cutbacks were envisaged as a means of overcoming difficulties with regional labour distribution, which severely threatened the fulfilment of the seven-year plan, we are entitled to assume that all the legal possibilities for diverting the discharged soldiers into regions with a labour shortage were exhausted.

In his speech of 14 January 1960, Khrushchev did not mention an organised regional distribution of demobilised soldiers and officers, he merely enumerated the trades in which the discharged soldiers could work.[122] On 16 January 1960, N. Salivakin (acting director of the labour and wages division of Gosplan) stated that "all of the demobilised 1.2 million soldiers will be employed in the economy, especially in the northern part of the country, in Siberia, the Urals and in the Far East".[123] With the exception of the Urals, these were all areas with a labour shortage.

A resolution of the Central Committee, published on 26 January 1960 in the Soviet press, explicitly prescribed the reintegration of discharged soldiers.[124] The introductory portion of the resolution reads as follows:

> "Integration of discharged military personnel must principally take place in industrial factories, at construction sites, in transport and in agriculture. One must give special attention to expediently complying with the wishes of those discharged soldiers who desire work and permanent residence in the northern regions, the Urals, Siberia, the Far East and the Kazakh Soviet Socialist Republic, as well as in kolkhozes and sovkhozes of the new and uncultivated areas of the RSFSR and the Kazakh Soviet Socialist Republic."[125]

The passage reveals the clear interest of the Soviet leading organs in dispatching the discharged soldiers to regions and economic branches suffering from a labour shortage. The text concerns itself almost exclusively (with the exception of one passage which deals with the professional retraining or further training of officers) with spelling out the needs which had to be met in accommodating discharged military personnel in the corresponding regions.

A number of privileges were extended to discharged military personnel who had accepted a labour contract for the above-mentioned areas: compensation of travel costs, an increased daily allowance for the duration of the journey, and privileges equivalent to those in the future place of employment. For officers and military personnel with long-term enlistment, their tour of duty at remote installations was credited to their term of employment, so that they would benefit from wage increases or other compensations in effect at their future place of employment. In addition, the local organs in outlying regions had the right to directly recruit military personnel who were ready to work in these areas.[126] The concluding passage of the Central Committee's resolution takes up once again the priority of diverting discharged military personnel into the Eastern regions of the Soviet Union:

> "The Central Committee of the Communist Party of the Soviet Union and the ministerial council of the USSR have recommended to the Central Committee of the VLKSM [Soviet Youth Organisation], in conjunction with a call for action issued according to earlier resolutions of the Central Committee of the Communist Party of the Soviet Union and of the ministerial council, to divert discharged military personnel *in the first place* [emphasis added] to the most important construction sites, factories and organisations of the Eastern region of our country."[127]

This resolution clearly shows the close connection between the troop reductions and problems of labour recruitment. Nevertheless, we cannot conclude that the troop cutbacks were carried out only because of the needs of regional labour and of the seven-year plan.

The Soviet perception of the international situation and the strategy of massive retaliation were the preconditions without which the troop reductions of 1960 could not have been carried through. We can therefore reasonably assert that the Soviet Union merely took advantage of the troop reductions in order to diminish its regional problems of labour recruitment. In contrast to preceding troop reductions, this time the problem of labour stood out more sharply, as is clear from the fact that during the troop reductions of the 1950s there were apparently no official directives aimed at channelling the labour released according to some prescribed plan. Although the material stimuli offered to discharged soldiers were not inconsiderable, they were only a partial guarantee that troop reductions would be effectively useful to the economy. The administration also had to solve social problems and the problem of training discharged military personnel for a civilian profession, if it was to integrate the discharged soldiers in the economic process. The efforts undertaken in this direction can be judged as an additional indicator of the administration's economic interest in the discharged soldiers.

On 20 January 1960, *Krasnaya zvezda* published a speech by Malinovski, then the Soviet defence minister, dealing with these questions.[128] Malinovski expected "certain difficulties" in the professional readjustment of the 250,000 officers, generals and admirals who were to be discharged — they accounted for more than a fifth of the total number of discharged men. According to Malinovski, party and government would concern themselves with job procurement and the retraining of officers in order to master this problem; in this respect, Malinovski appears to have been optimistic. He produced figures for the "successful accommodation" of more than 100,000 officers in the Moscow and Leningrad defence sub-districts during the period from 1954 to 1960. Although these two sub-districts cannot be regarded as representative of Soviet sub-districts as a whole, the following figures nevertheless illustrate how officer cadres could be integrated in the production process: 44,372 workers or white collar employees found a place in factories or offices; 17,292 became engineers or technicians; 10,374 found a place in the economic administration; 4,368 found a place in agriculture. The remainder of approximately 25,000 worked in the party. The Soviets, the trade unions, the Komsomol and in education. Of the 70,000 discharged officers of the Moscow defence sub-district, "over 40% occupied . . . responsible leading posts," which can be interpreted as meaning that about 60% of the officers had descended in the social scale as a result of their discharge. In reintegrating troops, non-commissioned officers and sergeants in industry and agriculture, hardly any difficulties were expected:

> "This problem [integration in the labour process] is easiest of all to solve in the case of troops and sergeants. . . . More complicated, and involving more responsibility, is the question of integrating officers and political workers into the

labour process. . . . We must handle these comrades with love and care."[129]

In Soviet accounts, the problem of utilising the financial resources freed by the troop cutbacks occupies a place second only to that of diverting the discharged military personnel into the critical regions. The financial side of the troop reductions of 1960 yields little for more extended analysis, since we know neither if the yearly savings announced by Khrushchev (1.6-1.7 billion rubles — a sum which would have corresponded to what the Soviets invested in 1959 in agriculture[130] — ever took effect, nor how the money was actually used.

In Western analysis, there is a tendency to ask not for what purposes the money was spent (particularly when a reorganisation of the Soviet armed forces is suspected) but for the reasons that could have motivated the Soviet Union to make such economies. Galay regards the decisive reason as the stresses upon the Soviet economy which resulted from the arms race and from economic assistance to China, to the socialist countries and countries of the third world.[131] The intention behind this position is obvious: the savings are interpreted merely as the result of over-extended international obligations on the part of the Soviet Union, and not as a worthwhile attempt to reduce defence costs for the benefit of society.

In his speech of January 1960, Khrushchev contradicted the Western assertion that the Soviet Union was carrying out its troop reduction "as a means of obtaining the resources to fulfil the seven-year plan. . . . We are undertaking a reduction in our armed forces not out of economic and financial weakness, but because of our strength and power."[132] Nevertheless, Khrushchev could not avoid simultaneously going into the economic advantages of the troop reductions: the yearly savings "of approximately sixteen to seventeen billion rubles" would be "a major support in fulfilling and overfulfilling our economic plans".[133] Sorin made the point even more clearly:

"One cannot hide the fact from the people that the savings of sixteen to seventeen billion rubles which the Soviet Union gains in connection with the reduction of its forces will be used as an essential support in fulfilling and overfulfilling the

seven-year plan for developing the economy of the USSR and
will serve to further increase the welfare of the Soviet
people."[134]

Khrushchev explained in detail how the freed resources were to
be used: "in raising the standard of living", "for further development of housing", "in reducing the working day".[135] The final
decision approved in a resolution of the Central Commitee of the
CPSU and of the cabinet council of the USSR "on measures for
increasing the production and improving the quality of food
products for the population."[136] This resolution, published in the
Soviet press on 27 January 1960, states:

> "The Central Committee of the Communist Party of the
> Soviet Union and the cabinet council of the USSR have
> decided that the financing of measures for expanding the
> production of food products for the population, as envisaged
> by the resolution, will be paid for by means of resources
> freed in connection with the reduction of expenditure on
> new military tasks, in accordance with the decree on substan-
> tial reduction of the USSR's forces which was passed at the
> fourth meeting of the Supreme Soviet."[137]

This planned utilisation of saved resources for the production
of consumer goods affected a sector in which Khrushchev had
promised to catch up with the United States. In spite of his
predictions, the development of the annual growth rate in
sector II was not so favourable: in 1959, the production of consumer goods only rose by 10.3% in comparison with the preceding year; in 1960 by only 7%, and in 1961 by only 6.6%.[138] In
his January speech, Krushchev himself made a substantial connection between the troop reductions, the increase in the production of consumer goods, and intersystemic competition over global
economic criteria of success. After he had enumerated the sectors
in which the financial resources freed through troop cutbacks
were to be utilised, he immediately went on to say:

> "It therefore turns out that the great armed forces in the
> countries of the military group opposing us are our involun-
> tary ally, which will facilitate the solution of our main prob-
> lem, that of surpassing the most highly developed capitalist

countries in all areas, both in science and in the production of machines and machine tools, as well as in the production of consumer goods and in satisfying human needs."[139]

The text obviously asserts that by keeping up their large armies (unnecessarily large from the Soviet military and strategic point of view) the capitalist states must put up with substantial social costs which worsen their performance in intersystemic competition; conversely, the Soviet Union improves its position by carrying out troop reductions. Troop reductions were therefore Khrushchev's means of carrying out his far-reaching plan for catching up with and overtaking the United States.[140]

We could corroborate the thesis that the Soviet Union had an evident economic interest in the troop reductions of 1960 if we could discover further attempts to make the military apparatus economically useful, or to hold down its costs. In fact, we can observe two such tendencies at the end of the 1950s. They concern the *shevstvo* system (best translated as "sponsorship") and the territorial system (also known as the "militia" system).

The connection between *shevstvo* and the military lay[141] in (a) the relationships between the military, its political organs and local civilian party organisations, and (b) the use of active military personnel in the civilian economy.[142] Kolkowicz distinguishes two stages in the development of *shevstvo* at the end of the 1950s: (a) from 1957, when the *shevstvo* system was reactivated, until 1959 (at this time, *shevstvo* was particularly political in nature); and (b) from 1959 on, when the economic functions of *shevstvo* stepped into the foreground.[143]

This enables us to deduce a connection between *shevstvo* and the seven-year plan ratified in 1959. In fact, one can find hints in the Soviet literature to support this thesis. In a collection of articles published in 1961, General N. Y. Kazakov declared that *shevstvo* was strongly intensified "in order to punctually fulfil the seven-year plan under conditions of national competition".[144] Another author in the same volume states that the "strengthening and expansion of friendly relations between soldiers and kolkhozniki" would be "of particular importance during the struggle to increase agricultural production."[145] One can assume that the *shevstvo* system carried economic weight; but one cannot determine to what extent this took place, since no statistical data exist for it. On the basis of the Soviet literature, Kolkowicz thinks it possible to infer a wide geographical expansion of *shevstvo*, and supposes that the use of military personnel for civilian purposes produced a high degree of organisation.[146]

The military construction units, which can be only conditionally classed with the conventional *shevstvo* labour, seem to have been "extremely useful to the economy":[147] partly because an essential part of its work served military purposes.[148] According to Soviet data for spring and summer 1961, these units built residential housing, factories, plants, electrical stations, railway lines, schools and hospitals.[149] This indicates that the military construction units were involved with the seven-year plan housing efforts, or that they had to be called in because of difficulties in the construction industry.[150]

Kolkowicz suspects that the economic reactivation of *shevstvo* was related to the need for labour, although he cannot find any direct proof in the Soviet literature.[151] A lead article in *Krasnaya zvezda* of 20 January 1960 — only six days after the announcement of the troop reduction programme — lends credibility to the idea that in 1960 *shevstvo* was considered as an additional possibility, along with troop reductions, for making economic use of military labour.

In his January speech, Khrushchev hinted that the troop reductions and the increased reliance upon the *shevstvo* system did not exclude the idea of using the economic capacities of conventional forces, and held out the prospect of reintroducing the territorial system in the future:

> "The government and the Central Committee of our party are considering and studying at the present time whether it would be purposeful to go over to the territorial system in building up our forces. . . . Glancing into the future, we can envisage that we would have units which could be called up according to the territorial principle. Their personnel would learn warfare without interrupting their production work."[152]

According to C. A. Linden, this was not the first time that Khrushchev had taken up the topic of the territorial system: in March 1958, he was supposed to have weighed up the possibility of gradually transforming the regular army into a territorial army. (At this time, the major outlines of the first seven-year plan would have already been known.) Khrushchev would already have seen this as a possibility for reducing the massive costs caused by the Soviet standing army.[153]

The economic advantages of the territorial system, which are backed up by the analysis of it as it was practised up to 1939 in the Soviet Union, are evident. Since the permanent staff of a territorial division did not amount to "more than 16% of the prescribed wartime strength", the economic costs of such a division were significantly lower than those of a cadre division. According to Galay, the costs amounted to approximately 34% of those of a regular division.[154] For the same reason, the territorial system did not absorb so much labour as did the previous traditional army system. According to the Ninth Party Congress of the Russian Communist Party (Bolsheviks) in 1920, the essence of the territorial system consisted in "bringing the army closer to the production process."[155] The party congress also stated:

> "The living labour power of certain economic regions is simultaneously the living combat force of certain troop units."[156]

Khrushchev's plan for converting to the territorial system — interpreted by Western analysts as representing a reduction in the strike power of the Soviet army[157] — meant that for the foreseeable future the aim was to employ conventional forces for their economic potential much more comprehensively than troop reductions.

Summary

The thesis on which this essay is based, namely that the military upgrading of the Warsaw Treaty Organisation and the Soviet troop reductions at the beginning of the 1960s were both dictated by the economic interests of the Soviet Union, is something we can only verify indirectly. The economic interest of the Soviet Union in troop reductions can be relatively clearly established on the basis of official declarations, in particular because of the precarious regional labour shortage which threatened the targets of the seven-year plan. On the other hand, it is substantially more difficult to define concretely the Soviet interest in a military upgrading of the Warsaw Treaty Organisation. The main reason was that the changes in military co-operation, as represented by the WTO arms build-up, also imply changes in the division of burdens; but this latter topic is obviously taboo in Eastern Europe. In order to reach the heart of the Soviet interest in an armaments build-up of the WTO, we chose a process of elimination, guided by the question: to what extent did the various factors in the international system influence the Soviet decision? We arrived at the conclusion that international relations, including the arms race and the development of strategy, could only have played a secondary role in the build-up of the WTO, although one must take them into account as a precondition for the build-up. The combination of troop reductions (as a disarmament measure) and the armaments upgrading of the WTO (as a build-up measure and thus, in an intersystemic context, as an example of rearmament) are only possible in a relatively relaxed international situation.

There is one other possibility for explaining the new distribution of military burdens which we have left out of account in this essay: the economic co-operation of Eastern European states in the Council for Mutual Economic Aid (CMEA). In the first place, this co-operation was in a state of disarray at the time of the WTO upgrading, and showed no signs of improvement; and secondly, one cannot directly decipher the economic consequences of military-political measures from the reactions of the CMEA. After we had broadly eliminated the possibility that factors in the international system had conditioned the WTO upgrading, the question remained: what could have motivated the Soviet Union to upgrade the WTO? We cannot give a foolproof answer with the material at our disposal. For various reasons, however, we believe that the Soviet economic interest in troop reduction had much in common with its interest in the WTO upgrading. Because we could find no sufficient intersystemic reason, we fell back upon internal social causes. Moreover, only conventional forces were affected in each case. This suggests that the Soviet Union compensated for its troop reductions, which were carried out primarily for economic reasons, by means of an upgrading of the conventional forces of its Warsaw Treaty partners, for reasons of security. We cannot ignore the fact that both events took place simultaneously.

The Soviet Union's economic interest in the WTO is also supported by the observation that after 1960, its WTO partners shared to a growing degree in the burdens of military defence. This can be observed with great clarity from the summer of 1961 on; the Soviet arms build-up, which also involved bringing the troop reduction programme to a halt, was accompanied by corresponding measures on the part of other WTO states, and military cooperation (in the form of manoeuvres, for example) were intensified.

NOTES

1. Cf. M. Garder, "Der Warschauer Pakt im System der sowjetischen Außenpolitik — eine Darstellung aus französischer Sicht", in *Europa-Archiv* (hereafter *EA*), 24 (1966), p. 895; E. Hinterhoff, "Es remort im Warschauer Pakt", in *Wehrkunde* II (1970), p. 555; R. Kolkowicz, "Spezifischer Funktionswandel des Warschauer Paktes", in *Außenpolitik* 1 (1969), pp. 11 and 17; R. A. Remington, *The Warsaw Pact* (Cambridge, Mass. and London 1971), p. 19; Th. W. Wolfe, "Die Entwicklungen im System des Warschauer Paktes", in *Osteuropa* (hereafter *OE*), 4 (1966), p. 210 ff.
2. Wolfe, *Soviet Power and Europe, 1945-1970* (Baltimore 1970), p. 148.
3. In the following essay we concern ourselves only with the WTO, leaving aside the system of bilateral treaties. Although this system covers the entire territorial area of the WTO, nevertheless as a whole it cannot replace a military alliance; cf. W. Gumpel and J. Hacker, "Comecon und Warschauer Pakt", in *Schriftenreihe der Bundeszentrale für politische Bildung* 73 (1966), p. 106.
4. Wolfe, *Soviet Power* . . ., p. 148.
5. Cf. V. Aboltin, *et al.*, *Politika gosudarstv i razoruzhenie*, vol. I: *SSSR — SShA i razoruzhenie* (Moscow 1967), p. 95.
6. V. A. Sorin, *Der Kampf der Sowjetunion für Abrüstung in den Jahren 1946 bis 1960 mit einer Ergänzung für die deutsche*

Ausgabe bis 1962 (Staatsverlag der DDR 1963), p. 243; an initial figure for 1955 could not be found in the East European literature.

7. Cf. J. M. Mackintosh, "The Evolution of the Warsaw Pact", in *Adelphi Papers* 58 (June 1969), p. 4; M. Czizmas, *Der Warschauer Pakt — Tatsachen und Meinungen* (Berne 1972), p. 67.

8. G. Glaser, K. Greese, T. Nelles and K. Schützle, "Zur Geschichte der Nationalen Volksarmee — Thesen", in *Militärgeschichte*, Beilage 4 (1973), p. 5.

9. H. Müller and M. Jakisch, "Geschichte und Bedeutung der sozialistischen Militärkoalition (1955-1965), in *Jahrbuch für Geschichte der UdSSR und der volksdemokratischen Länder Europas* 11 (Berlin 1967), p. 31. The Soviet literature deals with this aspect in a highly general form and then usually in close connection with the development of the different areas of the socialist world system. For this reason, in the following pages we have relied upon the East German literature; cf. S. P. Sanakov, *Mirovaya sistema sotsialisma* (Moscow 1968), p. 137; I. N. Mel'nikova, "Etapy razvitiya sotrudnichestva sotsialisticheskikh stran," in *Idei proletarskogo internationalizma — istochek druzhby i sotrudnichestva sotsialisticheskikh stran* (Uzhgorod 1972), p. 22.

10. A. Korbonski, on the contrary, is of the opinion that in the first ten years of its existence the WTO remained a "paper organisation"; see "The Warsaw Pact", in *International Conciliation* (May 1969), p. 15 f.

11. Cf. Remington, p. 72.

12. Cf. ibid., p. 79.

13. Wolfe, *Soviet Power* . . ., p. 150.

14. For example, until the beginning of 1960, the NVA was equipped with weapons from old stores of the Soviet army, cf. E. F. Pruck, "Die Streitkräfte der Sowjetunion und ihrer Verbündeten", in *OE* (1964), p. 675.

15. Cf. R. L. Garthoff, "Die Armeen der Ostblockstaaten", in *Osteuropäische Rundschau* 10 (1965), p. 13. The initial data are from F. Mischke, *Rüstungswettlauf* (Stuttgart 1972), pp. 205 and 449; cf. *The Military Balance 1971/1972* (London 1972), p. 63.

16. Gasteyger guesses that from 1961 on the WTO armed forces were already equipped with tactical missiles; cf. C. Gasteyger, "Reformbestrebungen und militärische Entwicklung im Warschauer Pakt", in *Ist der Osten noch ein Block?* (Kohlhammer 1967), p. 36.

17. D. R. Herspring, *East German Civil-Military Relations*: *the Impact of Technology 1949-1972* (New York, Washington, London 1973), p. 17 ff.
18. Ibid., p. 18.
19. Mackintosh traces the upgrading of the non-Soviet armed forces primarily to Grechko himself (cf. Mackintosh, "The Evolution . . .", p. 5 ff.).
20. Glaser *et al.*, "Zur Geschichte der Nationalen Volksarmee . . .", p. 14.
21. T. Nelles, "Mit schöpferischer Aktivität für die Stärkung der Verteidigungsfähigkeit des Sozialismus (1961-1965)", in *Militärgeschichte* 4 (1974), p. 472.
22. Ibid., p. 470; cf. H. Brünner, "Der proletarische Internationalismus — Grundzug der Erziehung der Armeeangehörigen zur sozialistischen Waffenbrüderschaft", in *Militärgeschichte* 4 (1974), p. 408.
23. Glaser *et al.*, "Zur Geschichte der Nationalen Volksarmee . . ." p. 14.
24. Ibid.
25. Cf. Gasteyger, p. 35.
26. Cf. Wolfe, "Die Entwicklungen . . .", p. 210; cf. also *The Warsaw Pact*: *Its Role in Soviet Bloc Affairs*. *Report of the Subcommittee on National Security and International Operations to the Commitee on Government Operations*, United States Senate, 89th Cong., 2nd Session (Washington, D.C. 1966), p. 9.
27. Ibid.; in this connection, we have left aside the Sino-Soviet conflict, since the military effects of the conflict at this time — in the form of Soviet troop concentrations at the border — cannot be detected. A report of the United States Senate in 1966 saw the WTO re-evaluation as an attempt by the Soviet Union to refute Chinese accusations that Moscow had had a disintegrating influence on the communist camp, c.f. *Report of the Subcommittee on National Security and International Operations . . .*, p. 12.
28. Cf. Müller and Jakisch, p. 40.
29. "Measures for increasing the defensive capability of the socialist coalition" were resolved upon; ibid., p. 39.
30. Cf. H. B. Moulton, *From Superiority to Parity* (Westport, N.Y. and London 1973), p. 51 ff.; J. M. Mackintosh, *Strategie und Taktik der sowjetischen Außenpolitik* (Stuttgart 1963), p. 251.
31. *Pravda*, 8 July 1961.
32. Cf. L. P. Bloomfield, W. C. Clemens and F. Griffiths, *Khrushchev and the Arms Race*: *Soviet Interests in Arms Control and Dis-*

armament 1954-1964 (Cambridge, Mass. 1966), p. 190 ff.

33. Th. Weingartner, *Die Außenpolitik der Sowjetunion seit 1945: eine Einführung* (Düsseldorf 1973), p. 40.

34. *Pravda*, 8 May, 1960; cf. A. L. Horelick and M. Rush, *Strategic Power and Soviet Foreign Policy* (Chicago and London 1966), p. 71.

35. Glaser *et al.*, "Zur Geschichte der Nationalen Volksarmee . . .", p. 14.

36. A. N. Bashkardin, *Ekonomicheskiy potentsial stran socialisticheskogo lagerya i ego znachenie v uprochenii ikh oboronosposobnosti* (Leningrad 1960), p. 52.

37. Cf. ibid., p. 51.

38. N. S. Khrushchev, "Razoruzhenie — put' k uprocheniyu mira i obespecheniya druzhby mezhdu narodami. Doklad na chetvertoy sessii Verkhovnogo Soveta SSSR 14 yanvarya 1960 goda", in *O vneshney politike Sovetskogo Soyuza, 1960 god*, vol. I (Moscow 1961), p. 17.

39. Brünner, "Der proletarische Internationalismus . . .", p. 408.

40. Superiority is still claimed today, although only in a very general form; cf. Heinz Hoffmann, in *Neues Deutschland*, 12 Dec. 1973: ". . . to make greater and ever greater use of the sources of the military superiority of socialism".

41. Khrushchev, "Razoruzhenie . . .", p. 13.

42. Cf. L. P. Ivashchenko, *Ekonomicheskiy potentsial stran sotsialisticheskogo lagerya i zadachi uproshcheniya ikh oboronosposobnosti* (Moscow 1959), p. 11 ff.; Bashkardin, pp. 11 f., 14, 25, 29.

43. Cf. Horelick and Rush, *The Political Use of Soviet Strategic Power*, Rand Corporation RM-2813 PR (Santa Monica, Calif., Jan. 1962), p. 61.

44. The Military Balance 1969/70 (London 1970), p. 55.

45. We cannot, in the framework of this contribution, go into the internal Soviet discussion about troop reductions in 1960; in relation to this question, cf., among others, R. Kolkowicz, *The Soviet Military and the Communist Party* (Princeton, N.J. 1967), p. 156 ff.

46. In 1961, just about the same time that the Soviet Union stopped troop reductions, the claim to superiority in strategic weapons was finally abandoned; cf. Horelick and Rush, *Strategic Power . . .*, p. 60.

47. The years 1959-60 show increased Soviet activity in the sphere of disarmament, causing A. Dallin to speak of the beginning

of a new phase in the Soviet Union's disarmament proposals (A. Dallin, *et al.*, *The Soviet Union and Disarmament: an Appraisal of Soviet Attitudes and Intentions* (New York 1964), p. 9. For the first time since 1932, the Soviet Union presented a "programme for general and complete disarmament" in 1959. V. A. Sorin connects this development with a relaxed international situation (Sorin, op. cit., p. 308).

48. Cf. M. Bornstein, "Economic Factors in Soviet Attitudes Toward Arms Control", in E. Benoit (ed.), *Disarmament and World Economic Interdependence* (Oslo), p. 62 f.
49. Khrushchev, "Razoruzhenie . . .", p. 36.
50. Bloomfield *et al.*, p. 92.
51. Horelick and Rush, *Strategic Power* . . . , p. 36 f.
52. Khrushchev, "Razoruzhenie . . .", p. 36.
53. *The Military Balance 1959-1964.*
54. Wolfe, *Soviet Power* . . . , p. 169.
55. *The Military Balance 1959-1973.*
56. According to Horelick and Rush, the construction of second-generation ICBMs was a closed question before 1960 (*Strategic Power* . . . , p. 37).
57. Ibid.
58. *Wolfe, Soviet Power* . . . , p. 142.
59. Khrushchev, "Razoruzhenie . . .", p. 49.
60. Sorin, p. 344.
61. Cf. V. S. Lel'chuk, "Industrial'noe razvitie SSSR v gody semiletki (1959-65)", in *Istoriya SSSR* 5 (1970), p. 14, 25.
62. *Die Streitkräfte der UdSSR, Abriß ihrer Entwicklung, 1918-1968* (Berlin [East] 1974), p. 635. [Translated from the Russian.] Cf. Malinovski's speech to the twenty-second party conference of the CPSU.
63. *Pravda*, 29 May 1960; cf. Malinovski in *Pravda* of 25 January 1962 (there exists "no necessity for increasing missile strike forces or weapons capacity"), and Khrushchev in *Pravda* of 2 October 1964 ("the defence of the USSR is at an appropriate level"), after Horelick and Rush, *Strategic Power* . . . , pp. 72, 101, 156.
64. Cf. A. Kirillov, "Predotvrashchenie voyny — vazhneyshaya problema sovremennosti", in *Kommunist vooruzhennykh sil*, no. 3 (1960); S. Kozlov, "O kharaktere vijn sovremennoi epokhi", in *Kommunist vooruzhennykh sil* 2 (1961).
65. The fact that there was also a strong tendency towards further reductions among the Soviet WTO partners was demonstrated

in 1963-64 by Rumania, at the beginning of a new phase of détente; the army's manpower was reduced and the period of military service shortened to sixteen months — evidently against the will of the WTO supreme command. Cf. Garthoff, p. 6.

66. Cf. H. Horn, *Europapräsenz und "flexible response": die amerikanische Stationierungspolitik in den sechziger Jahren*, doctoral diss. (Marburg 1974), p. 1-11.

67. R. Kolkowicz, "The Warsaw Pact: Entangling Alliance", in *Survey* (1969/70-1), p. 13.

68. Wolfe, *Sowjetische Militärstrategie* (Cologne and Opladen 1967), p. 20.

69. Cf. Gasteyger, p. 40.

70. Cited after B. Maurich, "Der XXII Kongreß der PKdSU und die sowjetische Militärpoltik", in *Wehrkunde* 2 (1961), p. 65.

71. Declaration of the participating states of the Warsaw Treaty, TASS report of 5 Feb. 1960, after B. Meissner (ed.), *Der Warschauer Pakt, Dokumentensammlung* (Cologne 1961), p. 188 ff.

72. Glaser *et al.*, "Zur Geschichte der Nationalen Volksarmee . . .", p. 16.

73. It must be emphasised that the present essay does not aim at analysing the implementation of the troop reduction of 1960, but only the planning of this troop reduction.

74. *Pravda*, 15 January 1960.

75. Malinovski in *Krasnaya zvezda*, 20 January 1960.

76. *Pravda*, 9 July 1961.

77. Cf. W. Hoffmann, "Der sechste Fünfjahresplan und die sozialökonomischen Veränderungen in der UdSSR", in *Osteuropa-Wirtschaft* (hereafter *OEWi* 1 (1956), p. 28; K. C. Thalheim, "Die Entwicklung der Wirtschaftsintegration im Ostblock", ibid., p. 11; Wolfe, *Soviet Power* . . . , p. 164.

78. *Vestnik statistiki* 6 (1958).

79. We can therefore dispense with Western theses which assert a general labour force surplus — or, as the case may be, unemployment — in the Soviet Union (e.g. R. R. Gill, "Volkszählung, Truppenkürzung und Arbeitskräfte", in *O.-P.* 6 (1960); "Bevölkerungsstatistik und Arbeitskräftepotential", in *O.P.* 6 (1959).

80. *SSR v tsiffrakh* (Moscow 1958), p. 31.

81. In his report on the seven-year plan, Khrushchev spoke of twelve million (cf. *Pravda*, 28 January 1959). The outline of the seven year-plan specified a figure of eleven million and a half

(cf. *Pravda*, 14 November 1958).

82. Eggers also establishes this connection: W. Eggers, "Der sowjetische Siebenjahresplan (1959-1965)", in *OEW* I (1959), p. 48.

83. See above, p. 178.

84. *Vestnik statistiki* 6 (1958).

85. For this problem, cf. D. Fischer, "Arbeitskräftefragen in der regionalen Wirtschaftsplanung der Sowjetunion", part 1, in *OEW* 1 (1966), p. 44 ff.

86. Cf. Sonin, *Aktual 'nye problemy izpol'zovaniya rabochei sily v SSSR* (Moscow 1965), p. 290 ff.

87. Soviet technical publications constantly refer to this problem and have attempted to work out proposals for improvement, cf. among others G. Vechkanov, "Povyshenie effektivnosti territorial'nogo pereraspredeleniya trudovykh resursov", in *Nauchnye doklady vysshei shkoly — Ekonomicheskie nauki* 5 (1969).

88. The Soviets today cite defective calculations in the area of labour planning as one of the main reasons for the failure of the seven-year plan. Cf. Lel'chuk, p. 15.

89. Cf. Fischer, p. 45.

90. In 1957, Wagenlehner asserted that a further rise in employment by means of an expanded mobilisation of women had been "eliminated". Cf. G. Wagenlehner, "Extensive und intensive Wirtschaftsform in der sowjetischen Planung", in OEW 2 (1957), p. 110.

92. Such as trade, insurance, science; cf. *Narodnoe khozyaistvo v 1963 godu*, p. 480 ff.

93. In particular, the Eastern regions, which suffer from an acute labour shortage, record a high percentage of unemployed women, something that can be traced back to one-sided industrialisation, cf. Fischer, p. 39 ff.

94. Cf. Knirsch, P., "Die Industrie der Sowjetunion im Jahre 1961", in *OEW* 2 (1962), p. 123.

95. P. Litviakov, *Demograficheskie problemy zanyatosti* (Moscow 1969) pp. 177, 181.

96. V. Smirnov, "Dvizhenie i ispol'zovanie trudovykh resursov sela (po nechernozemnoy zone RSFSR)", in *Nauchnye doklady vysshey shkoly — Ekonomicheskie nauki* 5 (1959).

97. Kolkowicz, *The Use of Soviet Military Labor in the Civilian Economy: a Study of Military "Shefstvo"*, Rand Corp. RM-3360 (Santa Monica, Calif., November 1962), p. 8 ff.

98. Cf. A. Kurski in *Voprosy ekonomiki*, no. 9 (1958), p. 22. The expected extent of the decline in the natural rate of labour growth can be gathered from the following data. 1955: a growth of 2.4 million; 1960: 0.3 million. Cf. *Socialisticheskiy vestnik* 4 (1956), p. 72.

99. Kolkowicz, *The Use of* . . . , p. 32.

100. See "Bevölkerungsstatistik und Arbeitskräftepotential", p. 283; Gill, p. 170.

101. Cf. the outline of the seven-year plan in *"Kontrollziffern* . . ." (see note 81 above), p. 482 ff.

102. Cf. Knirsch, p. 123.

103. Khrushchev, *Die Kontrollziffern* . . . , p. 47.

104. Khrushchev's report to the twenty-second Party Congress, in *Pravda* (18 October 1961), cited after Knirsch, p. 123.

105. As an example, one can cite the growth rate of labour productivity in industry:
Planned 1960: 6.0% (in comparison with the preceding year).
Realised: 5.4%
Planned 1961: 6.3% (in comparison with the preceding year).
Realised: 4.4%
Planned 1962: 6.6% (in comparison with the preceding year).
Realised: 5.9%
(data after Lel'chuk, p. 20).

106. Western investigations date the decline of the Soviet growth rate from the year 1959. To clarify the extent of the decline, we offer here some calculations of the Soviet growth rate between 1950 and 1961 (after Bornstein, table I):

	1950-58	1959	1960	1961
GNP	7%	3.9%	4.7%	6.1%
Industrial production	10.1%	8.1%	6.8%	6.4%
Agriculture	5.7%	4.1%	0.5%	8.6%

(The percentage values for 1950-58 are an annual average.)

107. Cf. D. Valentey. "Aktual'nye problemy narodonaseleniya v SSSR", in *Nauchnye doklady vysshey shkoly — Ekonomicheskie nauki*, no. 1 (1969), p. 53 ff.

108. Cf. Hoffmann, p. 31.

109. Another target of the seven-year plan was the further exploitation of Kazakhstan, which along with Siberia was to form the "third metallurgic basis of the USSR" and where, as in Siberia, there was an acute shortage of labour.

110. For example, the order of 10 February 1960 of the Presidium of the Supreme Soviet ("Ob uporyadoshenii l'got dlya lits,

rabotayushchikh v rayonakh krainego severa i v mestostyakh, priravnennykh k rayonam krainego severa", in *Sbornik zakonov SSSR 1938-61* [Moscow 1961], p. 575 ff.), which greatly enlarged benefits for the Eastern regions and offered additional material stimuli as a means of attracting labour to these regions.

111. Valentiy, p. A 212.

112. Perevedentsev in *Literaturnaya gazeta*, 10 March 1966, cited after W. Storck, "Das Arbeitskräfteproblem in der Sowjetunion", in *Sowjetstudien* 23 (1967), p. 24. The same is true for the entire Eastern region: "As can be seen from the reports, emigration from the Eastern regions continued during the years from 1956 to 1962. For example, during 1956-60 over 700,000 persons (including members of families) moved to Siberia as a result of recruitment, following the public appeal and even more frequently on their own initiative. But nevertheless the general rate of population growth in Siberia lay significantly below the natural, i.e. the number of people leaving Siberia exceeded that of people moving there." E. Manevich, "Vseobshchnost' truda i problemy ratsional'nogo ispol'zovaniya rabochei sily v SSSR", in *Voprosy ekonomiki* 6 (1965).

113. Manevich, p. 517. This corresponds to approximately 6% of the total wages bill.

114. *Voprosy ekonomiki*, no. 2 (1963), p. 158, after B. Lewytzky, "Zur territorialen Verteilung der sowjetischen Arbeitskräftereserven", in OE (1964), p. 367.

115. M. J. Sonin, *Vosproizvodstvo rabochei sily v SSSR i balans truda* (Moscow 1959), p. 167, after Lewytzky, p. 367.

116. Bashkardin, *Ekonomicheskiy potentsial* . . . , p. 31.

117. *Trud i zarabotnaya plata* 4 (1962), p. 36, after Lewytzky, p. 366. A more differentiated regional distribution, which confirms this table, can be found in Fischer, OEW 4 (1966), p. 295; it relies upon Soviet sources from 1963.

118. Lewytzky, p. 368 ff.

119. Ibid.

120. Cf. *Neues Deutschland*, 2 February 1960.

121. *Krasnaya zvezda*, 20 March 1959.

122. Khrushchev, "Razoruzhenie . . .", p. 51.

123. *Frankfurter Allgemeine Zeitung*, 16 January 1960.

124. *Pravda*, 26 January 1960.

125. Ibid.

126. Salivakin cites further privileges: "Credit for building a house, for which the state 'bears' half the cost; training of tractor operators . . . at state expense" (cited after *Frankfurter Allge-*

meine Zeitung, p. 3). But these benefits no longer show up in the Central Committee's resolution for voluntary labourers in the "virgin lands".

127. Emphasis ours; "in the first place" can be interpreted as expressing the expectation that discharged military personnel would not be attached to the general fluctuation trend.

128. Title of the speech: "Soviet Soldiers Pledge Allegiance to Resolution of the Supreme Soviet of the USSR."

129. Khrushchev, "Razoruzhenie . . .", p. 52 ff.

130. Cf. E. W. Schnitzer, "West European Comments on Soviet Posture as Presented in Khrushchev's Speech of 14 January 1960", Rand-Corp. RM-2557 (Santa Monica, Calif., 22 March 1960), p. 20.

131. Cf. N. Galay, "Social Problems in the Reorganisation of the Soviet Armed Forces", in *Bulletin of the Institute for the Study of the USSR* 4 (Munich 1960), p. 5. He overlooks the fact that at the beginning of 1960 the Soviet Union began to sharply reduce economic aid to China; cf. Mackintosh, *Strategie*, p. 159.

132. Khrushchev, "Razoruzhenie . . .", p. 50.

133. Ibid.

134. Sorin, p. 344.

135. Khrushchev, "Razoruzhenie . . .", p. 48.

136. Cf. Sorin, p. 344.

137. Ibid.

138. Soviet data after Knirsch, p. 22.

139. Khrushchev, "Razoruzhenie . . .", p. 48 ff.

140. Cf. Eggers, p. 43.

141. In the following discussion we rely upon the pamphlet of Kolkowicz, *The Use of* . . . The frequent reference to this work is due to the fact that it is the most well-founded investigation of this problem.

142. Ibid., p. 1 ff.

143. Ibid., p. 7; Kolkowicz believes he can observe a general turning away from the *shevstvo* system from the middle of 1962, cf. ibid., p. 36.

144. Ibid., p. 7, note 9.

145. Ibid., p. 7.

146. No geographical stress points can be detected from the enumeration of the regions, ibid., p. 14; thus the *shevstvo* system was directed at the military garrisons, and not vice versa.

147. Ibid., p. 18.

148. Ibid., p. 16; many military construction projects — for example,

bridges or streets — nevertheless also serve civilian purposes.

149. Ibid., p. 17; see in particular the article from *Krasnaya zvezda* (20 January 1960) below.
150. Cf. Khrushchev, *Die Kontrollziffern* . . . , p. 47 ff.
151. Kolkowicz, *The Use of* . . . , p. 5.
152. Khrushchev, "Razoruzhenie . . .", p. 53.
153. Linden, C. A., *Khrushchev and the Soviet Leadership 1957-1964* (Baltimore 1966), p. 68; in this case Linden gives no source.
154. Galay, p. 13 ff.
155. *Krasnaya zvezda*, 4 March 1960.
156. Ibid.
157. Cf. Pruck, E. F., in *OE* (1960), p. 7; Galay, p. 13.

INDEX

NOTES ON THE CONTRIBUTORS

Antonio Carlo teaches Industrial Law at the University of Cagliari, Italy. He is the author of several books on the USSR and has contributed to *Telos, International Journal of Sociology, Monthly Review* etc.

Egbert Jahn teaches at the J. W. Goethe University, Frankfurt. His publications include *Kommunismus — und was dann?* (Reinbek 1974).

Ekkehart Krippendorf is professor of International Relations at the John Hopkins University, Bologna. He is the author of *Die amerikanische Strategie* (Frankfurt 1970).

Rainer Rotermundt is on the staff of the German Society for Peace and Conflict Research, and his publications include *Das Denken John Lockes.*

Ursula Schmiederer is a director of the German Society for Peace and Conflict Research, and is the author of *Die sowjetische Theorie der friedlichen Koexistenz* (Frankfurt 1968).

Hillel Ticktin teaches at the Institute of Soviet and East European Studies at the University of Glasgow, and is editor of the review *Critique.*

Jutta and Stephan Tiedtke are on the staff of the Frankfurt Peace Research Institute, and their publications include "Die Rezeption der Ostpolitik in der UdSSR und DDR" (Opladen 1974), in E. Jahn and V. Rittberger (eds.), *Die Ostpolitik der BRD.*

DATE DUE

DATE DUE			
APR 8 1980			